F-80 SHOOTING STAR UNITS OVER KOREA

OSPREY
AVIATION

OSPREY FRONTLINE COLOUR

5

F-80 SHOOTING STAR UNITS OVER KOREA

Warren Thompson

First published in Great Britain in 2001 by Osprey Publishing
Elms Court, Chapel Way, Botley, Oxford, OX2 9LP

ISBN 1 84176 225 3

Edited by Tony Holmes
Page design by Mark Holt
Cutaway Drawing by Mike Badrocke
Origination by Grasmere Digital Imaging, Leeds, UK
Printed through Bookbuilders, Hong Kong

01 02 03 04 05   10 9 8 7 6 5 4 3 2 1

EDITOR'S NOTE

To make the Osprey Frontline Colour series as authoritative as
possible, the Editor would be interested in hearing from any
individual who may have relevant information relating to the
aircraft, units and aircrew featured in this, or any other, volume
published by Osprey Aviation. Similarly, comments on the edito-
rial content of this book would also be most welcomed by the
Editor. Please write to Tony Holmes at 10 Prospect Road,
Sevenoaks, Kent, TN13 3UA, Great Britain, or by e-mail at:
tony.holmes@osprey-jets.freeserve.co.uk

For a catalogue of all books published by Osprey
Military and Aviation please write to:

**The Marketing Manager, Osprey Direct, PO Box
140, Wellingborough, Northants NN8 4ZA, UK
Email: info@ospreydirect.co.uk**

**Osprey Direct USA, c/o Motorbooks International,
729 Prospect Avenue, PO Box 1, Osceola,
Wisconsin WI 54020
E-mail: info@ospreydirectusa.com**

Or visit our website: www.ospreypublishing.com

FRONT COVER *This impressive line-up shot of F-80Cs from the
8th FBG was taken on the sprawling flightline at Suwon Air Base.
The four aircraft closest to the camera (which will soon sortie
together as a flight) have just been loaded with 1000-lb GP
bombs that will be used to make rail cuts in North Korea. The jets
trimmed in red are from the 36th FBS (Robert E Crackel)*

BACK COVER *26th FIS pilot Lt Richard Escola prepares to fly a
practice intercept mission off the coast of Okinawa during the
late summer of 1950. His unit was the only one of the three
squadrons that made up the 51st FIW to remain behind on the
Japanese island to provide local air defence. The 16th and 25th
FISs, meanwhile, were fully committed to combat in Korea. Most
pilots assigned to the 26th saw action against the communists,
however, for they regularly undertook TDY (temporary duty) in
Korea. Here, they would fly combat missions with either the 16th
or 25th FISs – Escola completed numerous sorties with the
former unit (Richard Escola)*

TITLE PAGE *Lt Tom Owen paints the nose art on his The Beer
City Special in between missions. The red trim on his F-80
indicated that both he and his jet were assigned to the 8th FBG's
36th FBS. By the time this photograph was taken in 1953, the
8th FBG was the only F-80 fighter-bomber outfit left in-theatre –
two tactical reconnaissance squadrons were still equipped with
RF-80s as well (Tom Owen)*

TITLE VERSO PAGE *When the 45th TRS began converting from
the RF-51 to the RF-80, some of its aircraft were briefly painted
in a dull olive finish. Any tactical advantage this scheme gave the
recce jet was negated by the squadron's insistence on applying its
famous 'polka-dot' marking all over the aircraft's vertical stabiliser!
(Stan Newman)*

CONTENTS

LEFT *Aircraft from two of the 49th FBG's three squadrons have just rolled into their designated parking places at Taegu following the completion of yet another mission. The maintenance crews have already started to turn the aircraft around in preparation for their next strike sortie. Unmarked F-80 FT-822 is a replacement jet that has recently been flown in from Japan for one of the frontline squadrons. The aircraft would eventually receive its distinctive unit colours when time allowed the groundcrews to complete this non-essential task (Richard Immig)*

INTRODUCTION

During the final years of World War 2, a tremendous amount of research went into producing more sophisticated weapons. Two areas in particular would have a great impact on the world in the final half of the Twentieth Century – the atomic bomb and jet propulsion. The former was primarily used as a deterrent to keep world peace, whilst the latter was developed into a viable weapon which was mass-produced throughout the Cold War.

In the formative years of jet-propulsion, countless experimental aircraft designs were created in an attempt to make best use of this awesome power source. Few made it off the drawing boards, however, and even fewer made it into production. And with the Cold War fuelling still more development, those thypes that did reach the frontline were almost obsolete before they could achieve operational status.

In the United States, there were two promising entries into the new arena of jet fighters – the Bell P-59 Airacomet and the Lockheed P-80 Shooting Star. Bell's

entry (first flown in October 1942) was able to record a top speed of slightly over 400 mph, while the XP-80 (first flown in January 1944) broke the 500-mph barrier. The US Army Air Force (USAAF) saw great potential in the Lockheed airframe, and ordered 1000 as a result. At this time, in early 1944, it was apparent that the first operational jet fighter for the United States would be the F-80A. Sadly, it would not arrive in time to see action in World War 2.

As the P-80s came off the assembly line, they were delivered directly to operational squadrons. It was vitally important to the USAAF (soon to become the United States Air Force) that these aircraft remain in the news, thus selling the idea of an all-jet air force to the public. The success of this campaign would secure millions of dollars of appropriations from Congress.

This was a great coup for the USAAF, for in the immediate post-war years the battle-weary general public was not interested in pouring their tax dollars into war machines. Indeed, for such a major equipment change

to take place, the voters would have to be in favour of it. Fortunately for the air force, its publicity campaign enjoyed great success, and by late 1948 the Far East Air Forces (FEAF) was about to become the latest element within the USAF's all-jet force. The arrival of the Shooting Star signalled the end for the F-47 in the Philippines and for most of the F-51s in Japan.

Although military duty in Japan was considered to be one of the less strenuous postings in the USAF, FEAF units were nonetheless charged with keeping a weather eye on the political machinations of China and the USSR. With the latter superpower having successfully detonated an atomic bomb in 1949, there was always the possibility that the politically active Cold War could erupt into something much more deadly. The Soviets were well aware of the presence of F-80s in the Far East, but they were not aware of the jet's shortcomings which would be exposed during the first weeks of the Korean War.

The F-80-equipped groups controlled by the FEAF were the 8th, 35th and 49th FBGs in Japan, whilst the 51st Fighter Interceptor Group (FIG) was located on Okinawa and the 18th FBG flew out of Clark Air Base (AB), in the Philippines. Finally, the RF-80-equipped 8th Photo Reconnaissance Squadron (PRS) was also based in Japan.

Official FEAF records from June 1950 showed that there were a total of 360 operational F-80s in-theatre.

LEFT *The 8th FBS's Capt Joe Kepford poses by his F-80 on a relaxed 'down-day' at Misawa AB in May 1950 – just six weeks before the Korean War erupted. Typical of the many brave USAF pilots who made the supreme sacrifice in this bloody conflict, Capt Kepford was killed in action in September 1950. The air-to-ground role in which the F-80 was principally employed proved to be an extremely dangerous one, especially as the war ground on and the Chinese moved more sophisticated automatic weapons into North Korea (Marvin Johnson)*

The three wings that were based in Japan had all finished their upgrading to the newer F-80C models, although the 51st FIW, on Okinawa, still flew out-dated F-80As. On paper, at least, this was an impressive force, although it did little to deter communist aggression in Korea.

The units' areas of responsibility were as follows: the 8th FBW (35th, 36th and 80th FBSs) was based at Itazuke, and it covered the southern sectors of Japan; the 49th FBW (7th, 8th and 9th FBSs) was stationed at Misawa AB, up in the northern sector; and the 35th FBW flew out of Johnson AB, its 39th, 40th and 41st FBSs handling the central areas around Tokyo. On Okinawa, the 51st FIW controlled the 16th, 25th and 26th FISs. This unit

would end up furnishing two squadrons to the war effort, holding one back for defensive purposes. The 18th FBW, in the Philippines, would not see action with its F-80s, for the wing would revert back to F-51 Mustangs early on in the war. The FEAF's sole RF-80A unit was the 8th TRS, which was attached to the 35th FBG at Johnson.

These units would collectively create history during 37 months of conflict in Korea, proving that the F-80 was a most capable fighter-bomber. However, in the spring of 1950, these jet fighters were considered to be the ultimate aerial superiority aircraft in the Far East. Of course, American Intelligence had no knowledge of the existence of the MiG-15, and the impact it would have on air combat. After only five months of action over North Korea, the F-80 would be rendered obsolete with the appearance of the MiG-15.

In December 1950 USAF high command ordered F-86A Sabres into combat to stem the threat posed by the Soviet fighter, relegating the F-80 into the close air support and interdiction missions. Little did these top level decision makers realise that they had just 'unleashed a tiger' on the North Korean ground forces in the form of the Shooting Star.

Flown by highly motivated, and skilled, pilots, Lockheed's 'redundant' fighter would punish the invading forces all the way from the Yalu River down to the Pusan Perimeter.

Warren E Thompson
Germantown, Tennessee
March 2001

CHAPTER ONE
CRITICAL EARLY DAYS

Within hours of crossing the 38th Parallel into South Korea, the troops of the North Korean Peoples' Army (NKPA) had captured more territory than they could have hoped for. The communist troops had encountered practically no resistance, and with their conquest of the south nearing completion, few thought that the United States would bother coming to the rescue of the all but defeated South Korean army. However, nothing could be further from the truth, and the communist conquest of Korea in the summer of 1950 would eventually fail due to one major stumbling block – the USAF's Fifth Air Force, and its F-80s, F-82s and B-26s. However, the NKPA would continue to press south unmolested for the first 48 hours of the war.

During this period, bad weather over most of South Korea made it impossible for the Fifth Air Force to acquire accurate information on just what type of enemy equipment was using the roads, and how many troops were involved in the invasion. Unable to stop the communist advance, the Americans instead focused their attention on evacuating civilians from the Seoul area. This was accomplished via ship (out of Inchon Harbour) or C-54 from Kimpo airfield. Although FEAF HQ, in Tokyo,

was willing to do whatever was necessary to help complete the evacuation of US citizens from South Korea, its priority was to stem the enemy's advance. Central to achieving this aim were the FEAF's three F-80C groups.

When the invasion was launched on 25 June 1950, the closest of these units to South Korea was the 8th FBG. It was immediately ordered to provide sufficient fighter cover to ensure that the evacuation of the Seoul area was completed without interference from the North Korean Peoples' Air Force (NKPAF). On the 26th, most US citizens and certain key South Korean civilians boarded a Norwegian freighter in Inchon Harbour and were shipped to safety.

The remaining personnel were assembled at Kimpo airfield in the early hours of the following morning and flown out by a fleet of USAF C-54s. Covering the operation was the 35th FBS, whose pilots were forced to fly above thick cloud which had blanketed the area since the start of the invasion. This operation ran smoothly until midday, when all hell broke loose.

Flying below the cloud (which sat at an altitude of about 1000 ft) was a flight of F-82 Twin Mustangs, and

they duly intercepted and shot down three Soviet-built fighters. This was an advance force leading a larger formation of Ilyushin Il-10 attack aircraft, which were in turn set upon by the F-80s.

Less than 24 hours into the crisis, it was already becoming evident that the F-80 had one glaring short-coming – it did not have the range to loiter on patrol for any useful length of time. 8th FBG pilot Lt John D McKee encountered this problem on the second day of the war;

'At about 0230 hrs on 26 June, I was summoned to squadron ops. Apparently, there was some sort of emergency developing, and they wouldn't tell us much. At the briefing, I was told that I would lead a flight of two F-80s from Itazuke over to the Pusan area, where I would contact ground control. In doing so, we were instructed to remain on orbit until our fuel ran low. We were simply told that South Korea was being attacked from the north and no further details were provided.

'We completed our mission without incident and returned to Itazuke, where confusion still reigned. We refuelled, and I was told that I was to lead a two-ship patrol to Seoul at 0800 hrs.

'Soon after we had established our orbit, a ground controller radioed for us to report any military activity. At that moment, I heard another F-80 pilot further north, radio for permission to engage an airborne Yak-9.

'Things were starting to heat up. As I looked over the roads, I spotted a convoy of trucks and tanks trying to cross the Inchon River (north to south). I also noted that the troops were building a pontoon bridge, and that the convoy was at a standstill. This wasn't just any minor troop movement, for the convoy was nearly two miles long!

'I requested permission to fire on the column, and it took nearly ten minutes to get a response! My fuel only allowed me to spend 13 minutes over the area, and I had had to wait ten minutes to get the approval. I later learned that the delay was caused by the many commands that the request had to pass through for approval. There was a lot of confusion on the ground as to where friendly troops were located. Finally, we were cleared to fire.

'With seconds ticking off, I directed my wingman to strafe the northern end of the convoy from east to west, and I would do the same on the southern end. The purpose of this tactic was to knock out trucks at either end of the convoy, thus restricting the movement of the remaining vehicles. We encountered no AA fire throughout the attack, allowing us to take our time and accurately strafe the trucks. We set numerous fires and observed a number of explosions on our passes. We also noted heavy troop movements to the north and north-east of the convoy, but we were too low on fuel to engage these targets.

'Due to our low fuel state, we were given a straight-in approach to Itazuke. We had been among the first to witness the enemy activity on the roads.'

The first aircraft to fly dedicated reconnaissance sorties over the invading North Korean forces were the camera-equipped RF-80As of the 8th TRS. Poor weather had restricted such overflights until the morning of 28 June, by which time the FEAF was desperate for some accurate intelligence on the crisis.

The unit had been notified before nightfall on the 27th that the weather was due to break the following day,

ABOVE *Weapons expended over the frontline, yet another 80th FBS F-80C is seen heading back south to Itazuke. When the 80th's two sister squadrons (35th and 36th FBSs) reverted to flying the F-51, the unit was transferred to the F-80-equipped 51st FIG, which in turn restored the latter group to full strength (typically three squadrons). When the 35th and 36th FBSs switched back to F-80s, they were rejoined by the 80th FBS under the control of the 8th FBG (Russ Rogers)*

LEFT *Once the F-80s were able to operate out of South Korean airfields, they became far more effective in the ground attack role. Following the North Koreans' retreat back across the 38th Parallel, the first major base freed up for F-80s was at Taegu. This photograph was taken at the airfield just days after the 8th FBG had flown in from Itazuke AB. The sunburst marking on the jets' vertical stabilisers was the trademark of the group (Francis Clark)*

INSET *This 49th FBG F-80 was caught by a large-calibre anti-aircraft shell whilst on a strafing run at low-level in a valley – the gun was sited in the side of the valley wall. Hitting the aircraft squarely in the vertical stabiliser, the shell passed through the F-80 without causing any irreparable damage. If the round had hit home just a split-second sooner, however, it could have knocked out the engine or gravely wounded the pilot. The F-80 made it safely back to Taegu AB, where it was repaired in time to participate in missions flown the following day (Tom Gerzel)*

and it was duly ordered to immediately send four RF-80As down from Yokota AB to Itazuke. The honour of flying the first official photo-reconnaissance mission of the war would go to Lt Bryce Poe, who took off from Itazuke in the early hours of the 28th. The weather over the 38th Parallel was rapidly clearing, and he was able to take some truly revealing photographs. Later that day, he flew a second mission over the same area, and noted that the roads were littered with burning trucks and equipment. Yet despite the F-80s and F-82s having worked the convoys over with both bombs and rockets, the overwhelming tide of the invasion had not been slowed at all.

By the third day of the conflict, it was obvious that the F-80 did not possess the fuel capacity to allow it to carry heavy ordnance over long distances from bases in Japan to the Korean frontline. Although pilots could fly to and from the battlefield, they could not spend time seeking out targets. When the 'all-jet' force had become operational in the Far East, no one envisaged that it would have to fight such a conflict over great distances just months after the re-equipment had been completed. This problem had to be addressed immediately, and fortunately for the FEAF, the 49th FBW had the answer.

In 1949 the wing had won the Far East Gunnery Meet, giving it the opportunity to compete with other USAF units at Nellis AFB. In order to reach the Nevada base, a long over-water flight had to be completed. A plan had to be devised to get the 'short-legged' F-80s all the way across the Pacific to the US, and one of the pilots who came up with a solution was the 9th FBS's Lt Edward R 'Rabbit' Johnston;

'Lt Robert Eckman and I had finished with top honours at the big Far East Gunnery Meet, and we felt that we would have a better chance of winning at Nellis if we were able to take our own aircraft. The big problem was how to complete the long leg between Shemya Island, off Alaska, to Anchorage. We suggested that two additional centre sections be added to the current wing tip tanks, which would boost our fuel capacity by at least 110 gallons in each tank. The fabrication and assembly was very easy, requiring only the extension of the large bolts that held the three sections of the normal tank together.

'We then flew a series of profiles missions and proved beyond a doubt that we had more than doubled the range of the F-80! Unfortunately for us, the "brass" at HQ AF Materiel Command feared that the heavier tanks would stress the wings, and they told us to shut the project down, as it was untested and not worth the risk.

'But, in the desperate days of late June 1950, Gen Earle Partridge, Commander of Fifth Air Force, overrode the veto and ordered the big "Misawa" tip tanks to be manufactured as fast as possible so that all of the F-80s committed to the Korean War could use them. You had to be very careful when pulling Gs in strafing and dive-bombing runs because of the extra stress put on the entire apparatus. More than one pilot got in trouble when one of the tanks failed to feed and he couldn't jettison it.

'Landing an F-80 with 265 gallons of fuel hanging on one wing was a dicey proposition. As crazy as it may seem, the only way out of this situation was to roll the canopy back, take out your 0.45-cal pistol and shoot holes in the full tank!'

BELOW These F-80s are seen bombed up ready for serious business during the defence of the Pusan Perimeter, this photograph being taken on the 35th FBS ramp at Itazuke AB. The F-80s parked in the distance to the left of this shot belong to the 9th FBS (49th FBG). All Shooting Stars committed to the war effort at this early stage were based at Itazuke (Francis Clark)

'The extended range that these tanks gave the F-80 meant that pilots were free to roam the Korean peninsula and perfect the art of the ground strafing and bombing.'

Lt Ed Jones of the 80th FBS was one of the handful of pilots who actually had to resort to shooting at his own tip tanks. He remembers;

'On one mission, we were heading north towards the bomb line and I could not get either of my tip tanks to feed. After relaying this problem to my flight leader via the radio, he told me to jettison my bombs and external tanks and head back to base. Upon punching the jettison button, all of the right side let go, but nothing happened on the left side! I was heading south at the time and getting close to our base at Suwon.

'We had been told that you could not land the F-80 with full tanks on one side and empty ones on the other because the jet could not be trimmed out enough to make it safe.

'I decided to use my 0.45-cal pistol and try to shoot a hole in the left tank. I cranked the canopy back and got my pistol out. I shot two holes in the front of the tank and fuel began to stream out. After a short while, enough had leaked out to trim the aircraft out. I lined up with the runway and made a smooth landing, and after rolling down the strip for about 2000 ft, the control tower came on the radio and told me that my left tip tank had just come off, and that it was bouncing down the runway behind my aircraft!

'It had been a frustrating day because my mission had been such a bust. However, on the positive side, my jet

was quickly repaired, and it went on to complete many more missions.'

With the war less than two days old, the 49th FBG was called into the action from its base at Misawa. The first of its squadrons thrown into action was the 9th FBS, which had been deployed to Komaki on exercise at the time of the invasion. It was immediately ordered to fly to Itazuke to join the 8th FBG, the F-80s flying in on the morning of 27 June. Meanwhile, at Johnson AB the 35th FBG committed the 39th and 40th FBSs to the crisis.

Aside from having to cope with the F-80's inadequate range, units were also struggling to find 7000-ft paved runways from which to operate. A fully loaded Shooting Star needed every foot of this in order to build up sufficient speed to take off safely. Only four bases in Japan boasted such runways, and in Korea the situation was even worse – Pusan AB was the sole facility with such a runway, and it was in the process of being 'beaten to death' by the heavy transport traffic rushing troops and equipment into Korea.

This meant that Itazuke was the closest base to the frontline, although it too rapidly became overcrowded, forcing the 35th FBG to move its two squadrons from Yokota to Ashiya. The 49th FBG's 8th and 9th FBSs were allowed to remain at Itazuke, however, increasing the number of available F-80 squadrons to seven.

Due to range restrictions, Shooting Star pilots relied exclusively on the aircraft's six 0.5-in machine guns when engaging the enemy between 28 June and 6 July. By choosing not to carry external ordnance, units reduced

ABOVE *A fully-loaded F-80 of the 16th FBS departs an undisclosed base with the aid of JATO bottles. With the runways at Suwon and Taegu being too short for Shooting Stars to get airborne in this configuration during the hot summer months, JATO became a necessity. Note that the pilot has already started to retract the jet's undercarriage, despite the aircraft having been airborne only a matter of seconds (Mary Etta Johnson)*

the overall weight of their F-80s, which in turn meant that pilots could eke out a few more precious minutes over the frontline.

A typical mission would see a Shooting Star fly 310 miles from Itazuke to Han River, and back again. Once over enemy territory, pilots found that the roads were packed with enemy troops and vehicles. Rather than rushing into take their target by surprise, F-80 pilots preferred to orbit the area at 10,000 ft in order to make sure that there were no enemy aircraft lurking in the area. As fuel began to get low, they would dive down and strafe anything that was moving. Using up their ammunition, the pilots would then head south again for Itazuke to refuel.

Fortunately, there were enough F-80s committed to the conflict to allow the FEAF to overfly the constantly changing frontline (in flight strength) every 20 minutes, which meant the pressure was kept on the communists throughout the hours of daylight.

When preparing for the invasion of South Korea, the NKPA had failed to impress upon its personnel the deadly effectiveness of airpower when used correctly. The FEAF was the only air arm of note in the region, and perhaps senior officers had hoped that the US military would not intervene in the conflict. Whatever the case, American pilots noted that on low-level strafing runs enemy troops would stand up in trucks and fire their rifles at the oncoming fighter-bombers! Seconds later, they were engulfed in a massive explosion or a fiery shroud of napalm. This cost the North Koreans the lives of literally thousands of valuable troops, but even with this fatal flaw in its tactics, the NKPA kept pushing south completely unchecked. Within a few weeks, the infamous Pusan Perimeter was beginning to take shape, as the United Nations' forces fought to keep a toehold on Korean soil.

In mid-July, the American presence in the air over Korea took a dramatic turn with the arrival in Japan of the aircraft carrier USS *Boxer*. Aboard the vessel were 134 F-51D Mustangs pulled from various reserve and air guard units in the US (see *Osprey Frontline Colour 1 - F-51 Mustang Units over Korea* for further details). The fuel-hungry F-80s would be affected most by this sudden increase in the number of F-51s in-theatre. Changes commenced immediately, for on 10 July the 35th FBG's 40th FBS exchanged its Shooting Stars for Mustangs. Days later the 18th FBW (at Clark AB, in the Philippines) left its F-80s behind and moved to Korea to fly F-51s.

The 8th FBG would also eventually see two of its units (the 35th and 36th FBSs) revert to piston power, although not before they had flown their F-80s on numerous missions deep into North Korea. One such mission, undertaken on 19 July, all but finished off the NKPAF.

On this day an RF-80 had performed an early-morning photo-run over the main communist airfield at Pyongyang. Once back in Japan, its processed film revealed at least 25 aircraft dispersed among trees on the edge of the field. A strike was immediately ordered, and within an hour the 8th FBG had launched seven F-80s from Itazuke to bomb the airfield.

The attacking pilots found the aircraft still hidden amongst the trees, and they duly launched into a series of deadly low-level strafing passes. No fewer than 14 Yak fighters and Il-10s were destroyed, and the remaining aircraft heavily damaged. Bomber Command was also informed, and the next morning B-29s cratered the runways at Pyongyang, temporarily rendering the airfield inoperable.

The 35th and 36th FBSs gave up their F-80s on 11 August, while the 80th FBS retained its jets. The now surplus Shooting Stars did not sit idle for long, however, for they were duly absorbed by the 49th FBG.

These equipment changes were made solely because the F-51s could operate from numerous Korean bases and the F-80s could not. Closeness to the frontline also meant that Mustang pilots could loiter for an hour or more over targets deep in North Korea. And once they had completed their mission, the veteran fighters could fly back to their bases, reload and then sortie on a second or third mission all in the same day!

Eventually, F-80 units would also be able to mirror this performance following the establishment of hastily-built bases in Korea, although for the time being the ratio of piston-engined fighters to jets had significantly changed within the FEAF following the arrival of the Mustang. Indeed, following all these equipment changes only four F-80 squadrons remained directly committed to the war. And one of these – the 49th FBG's 7th FBS – was held back in Japan due to limited airfield space in Korea. The FEAF now realised that it was short of Shooting Star units in-theatre, so it chose to bring in another fighter bomber group from Okinawa.

On 22 September (a few days after the famous Inchon Landing by the US Marines) the 51st FIW was ordered to send two of its three units to Itazuke, from where they would be sent into action over Korea. The 16th and 25th FISs duly moved bases, leaving the 26th FIS behind on Okinawa to perform air defence duties.

The timing of this move was perfect, for the airfields in South Korea that had been overrun by the communists in the first days of the war had now been recaptured by UN troops and made available to the F-80 units. Able to launch from bases appreciably closer to the frontline, pilots now enjoyed far greater loiter time over key targets in the north, thus increasing the effectiveness of the F-80s.

Nicknamed the 'Screamin Demons', the 7th FBS moved from Misawa to Itazuke on 14 August – it was in turn replaced by the 9th FBS 'Iron Knights'. The 7th was well stocked with aircraft at this point in the war, and it brought with it no fewer than 33 F-80s to Itazuke. Before the sun had set on its first full day in the frontline, the unit had logged 37 sorties.

The unit had arrived in the frontline just as the Pusan Perimeter was feeling the squeeze of an all out NKPA attack to rid Korea of UN troops. This meant that there was no shortage of targets to hit, and on this first day alone, the unit expended 27,000 rounds of ammunition and 43 rockets – no bombs could be carried due to the distance that separated Itazuke from the target area. The official records for the 7th FBS show that the unit just about duplicated these figures on its second day of combat.

Despite being unable to carry bombs, the F-80s nevertheless caused considerable damage within the enemy strongholds at Kumchon, Taejon, Taegu, Sinju and Pyongyang.

As impressive as the efforts of the fighter-bombers were during the month of August, these missions failed to slow the enemy's advance into South Korea. Supplies continued to head southward during daylight hours, thus proving that the NKPA could easily make good the losses it had suffered at the hands of UN air power. Only when these losses became more difficult to sustain would the communists resort to the nocturnal movement of supplies – and this would occur only after the Chinese Army had entered the war.

BELOW *This unusual photograph was taken just days before the war started, and it shows a flight of F-80s from the 35th FBS flying past Mount Fuji. Most F-80 squadrons based in Japan pre-war had ample opportunity to fly over the country's most photographed landmark (Harris Boyce)*

The first F-80 combat loss of the war was suffered by the 8th FBG on 30 June. The 36th FBS's Lt Charles Wurster (who also scored a 'kill' on this day) remembers;

'Whilst we were working over the marshalling yards at Seoul, squadronmate 1Lt Edwin T Johnson received three direct hits in the nose and canopy from 20 mm anti-aircraft fire. The third round hit the jet's canopy beside his head, and he instinctively moved the stick forward. This change of course was just enough to make him fly through several cables that had been strung out over the yard by the North Koreans. Despite hitting the cables doing 500 mph, Johnson still managed to climb away from the target area and steer a course for home.

'Once safely out of reach of the flak batteries, he surveyed the damage to his jet. Both of its tip tanks and the end of each wing had been torn off. Furthermore, both wings had three or four gashes sliced almost all the way through them. Most of his canopy and windscreen were also gone, and the upper half of his rudder and vertical stabiliser had been sliced away, as had half of the left elevator and horizontal stabiliser.

'Lt Johnson climbed up to 13,000 ft, where he had his wingman check over the damage. The latter reported that the entire tail section was waving back and forth as though it was about to fall off! Lacking an ejection seat, Johnson decided to bail out, for he was convinced that if the tail did fall off, he probably would not have been able to get out of the tumbling aircraft.

'He received painful, but not serious, wounds when he struck the right horizontal stabiliser as he fell away from the cockpit. Johnson landed near to Suwon, and he was picked up and airlifted back to Itazuke that same afternoon! The F-80 was a rugged airframe that succeeded in getting a lot of shot-up pilots back to their home base.'

Another veteran of these early Shooting Star missions was Lt Col Clure Smith, CO of the 25th FBS. His squadron arrived in Korea from Okinawa in the wake of the Inchon invasion, the unit initially benefitting from being able to operate from the recently-liberated Kimpo AB;

'Following 250 missions in fighter aircraft during two wars, I hardly remember any specific mission! When the Chinese kicked us out of Kimpo AB, and we moved back to Tsuiki, in Japan, we encountered problems with our fuel load. We couldn't fly to Korea and spend enough time over the target area at low altitude and still get back to Japan. Our 165-gallon tip tanks were replaced with the new elongated 265-gallon tips, and these would some-times drag along the runway and leak.

'With the Chinese in the war, our targets changed. We had to destroy the bridges across the Yalu River, plus all of the rail lines, so they loaded us with 1000-lb bombs instead of the regular 500 "pounders", plus we could also carry four 5-in rockets.

OPPOSITE *Within hours of the 25th FIS being ordered to move to Itazuke from Okinawa, the squadron flightline had become a hive of activity – the 51st FIW would send two of its three units to war. Standing by his aircraft is 25th FIS CO, Lt Col Clure Smith. This jet is in the process of having its guns checked, and then loaded with ammunition, thus allowing it to be ready to fly its first sortie upon arriving at Itazuke. The unit moved to mainland Japan in the wake of the Inchon Landing in September 1950 (Clure Smith)*

Col Stanton T Smith, CO of the 49th FBG, prepares to climb aboard his F-80C (FT-500) at the start of yet another combat mission. This photograph was taken at Itazuke AB in July 1950. Note the jet's distinctive three-colour nose cone, which indicated that it was the group CO's F-80. Each colour denoted one of the squadrons (7th, 8th and 9th FBSs) within the group (Jack Jenkins)

RIGHT *1Lt John Dawson poses alongside the F-80C assigned to the commander of the 25th FIS. This photograph was taken just after the unit had arrived back on South Korean soil following the halting of the Chinese Offensive in the spring of 1951. The 25th FIS's pilot roster was constantly bolstered by a steady influx of personnel from the 26th FIS, who were posted in from Okinawa on TDY (John Dawson)*

'Now, our jets are carrying two 265-gallon wing tanks, two 1000-lb bombs and four 5-in rockets, and there is no way that the F-80s are going to get off the ground under their own power, so the groundcrew mount single JATO (jet-assisted take-off) rockets on either side of the fuselage. We were told that these would help us get airborne before we ran out of runway, and I remember praying a lot as I rolled past the point of no return!'

Some of the 5-in rockets that were initially used had been left over from the Pacific campaign in World War 2. Stored for the intervening five years, a number of the rockets had had their fins badly bent out of shape, and these duly flew erratically once fired! On the few occasions that they flew true to aim, the results achieved were impressive – even against Soviet-built tanks.

Here, 16th FBS pilot Lt Carl Ebneter recalls his experiences with the High-Velocity Aerial Rockets (HVARs);

'On one mission, I attacked a T-34 tank with two rockets that did not hit the mark, so I decided to strafe them with my guns. I forgot to reset my gun sight, and on a long firing pass I could not see any hits. About 200 yards beyond the tank a large explosion occurred, and I realised that my guns had overshot the tank and hit an ammo dump. It was an example of dumb luck and marginal marksmanship!

'A short time later, we were launching from Kimpo and I was leading the second element. We were going after a supply route. As I pulled up after my first strafing pass, I noticed a gun position firing at me from a ridge. I decided to fire two of my rockets at him. As I fired, one of the rocket motors exploded, smashing the drop tank beneath my left wing. It also took out the firing and arming wires for the adjacent rocket, leaving me with a hot rocket and badly shaking aircraft (and pilot).

'After slowing down below 200 mph, the buffeting stopped. My flight leader came underneath for a close look at the damage, and he told me that I had two holes on the underside of the wing. We debated trying to salvo the rocket, but decided not to as it looked secure. I also knew that salvoing did not always work, and when the rocket failed to drop in flight, it usually released on landing. In that event, my only means of escape was to eject, for the rocket would have exploded. Needless to say, I made one of my smoothest landings ever!'

LEFT The key to the F-80's effectiveness once the Chinese entered the war was the fast turnaround, with units flying as many sorties as the maintenance people could support. These heavily-loaded 'Screamin Demons' from the 7th FBS have been rearmed with napalm and rockets for their afternoon mission against suspected troop concentrations. This deadly combination was also effective against enemy tanks that were caught out in the open
(Frederic Champlin)

MAIN PICTURE *For several months in mid-1950, Itazuke was almost certainly one of the world's busiest air bases. It was undoubtedly home to more F-80s than any other airfield in the USAF. These red-trimmed machines were assigned to the 25th FIS, and they are seen being loaded with 5-in rockets. Note that each jet is also fitted with stretched 'Misawa' tanks, which again came into their own following the Chinese offensive of late 1950 when the Korean-based F-80 units had to hastily flee back to Itazuke (Frank Durkee)*

INSET *A grim reminder of just how close the war came to being over before Christmas 1950. This was the scene at Pyongyang Main airfield in October 1950, when the North Korean capital was captured by UN troops. The gutted hulks of two F-80s from the 51st FIW can be seen amongst the debris of war. Within a few weeks of this photograph being taken, UN forces were in full retreat out of North Korea in the wake of the Chinese offensive (Homer Hansen)*

OPPOSITE TOP *Lt Col Evans Stephens, CO of the 16th FBS, poses on the flightline at a forward base in South Korea. He was heavily involved in the first jet-versus-jet action with the MiG-15 in early November. His wingman on that mission was Lt Russell Brown, who was credited with the MiG kill (Evans Stephens)*

LEFT ABOVE *The old fighter-bomber adage, 'the lower the better' is graphically demonstrated by this photograph. An anonymous 9th FBS pilot poses proudly beside his battered F-80 at Taegu in the late summer of 1950. It appears as if the jet might have had a close encounter with a tree. Despite suffering significant damage (particularly to the starboard air intake), the Shooting Star nevertheless made it safely back to base, where it was repaired and restored to flying status within 48 hours of this photo being taken (Al Coleman)*

LEFT BELOW *Maintainers had their hands full repairing battle-damaged F-80s in time for the unit's next mission. This 8th FBS machine seems to have suffered a nose gear failure on landing at Taegu, which has necessitated the removal of the whole forward section of the jet. The repair work is already well underway, and chances are that the F-80 was ready to fly another mission within 48 hours of the accident taking place. The other F-80 shown in this view is a blue-trimmed 7th FBS jet, this unit being co-located at Taegu in the late spring of 1951 (Nat King)*

Not all battle-damaged F-80s made it back to base. This 80th FBS aircraft sustained numerous flak hits whilst on a mission in the spring of 1951, and although the pilot was able to nurse his jet back to the Wonju area, he knew he could not get it down in one piece. He therefore elected to bail out, and the aircraft struck the ground just minutes later (William Rockwell)

RIGHT *This aircraft was the assigned mount of Lt George Rutter of the 25th FIS, and it is seen being rearmed with a full load of 0.5-in ammunition. Rutter would continue his career in the USAF post-war, eventually attaining the rank of major general (George Rutter)*

BELOW *Maj Mike Horgan of the 8th FBS checks the filler cap pressure seal on the right wingtip tank of his F-80 during his pre-flight walkaround. Behind him, service crews top off the fuselage tank. This photograph was taken in December 1950 – just as the Chinese entered the war, forcing UN fighter-bomber squadrons to fly literally around the clock in an effort to stem the seemingly unstoppable communist invasion (Marvin Johnson)*

CHAPTER TWO
ESTABLISHING AIR SUPERIORITY

When the all-jet F-80 force was established in the Far East in 1949, its sole mission was to achieve air superiority in the region in the event of war. And although the F-80s were capable of carrying bombs, little emphasis was placed on the ground attack role. The Shooting Star units were strictly in-theatre to provide air defence. The jet's modest range presented few problems when performing this mission for each group defended a set area, and all of them trained hard to react quickly to any incursions of their airspaces, intercepting intruders within a matter of minutes. The idea of carrying a heavy load of ordnance across the Sea of Japan and then several hundred miles inland into Korea had never even been contemplated, let alone practiced, by the F-80 units pre-war.

With the all-jet fighter interceptor force signalling the demise of the F-51 Mustang within the FEAF, the role of aerial interceptor was placed almost entirely in the hands of the F-80. The only other heavily-armed fighter type in-theatre was the all-weather F-82G Twin Mustang.

The latter machine was a superb dogfighter with substantial firepower, although its aircrews did not spend time practising group fighter tactics. Their all-weather mission meant that they were loners, with each crew working a certain sector in total darkness. This left Lockheed's F-80 as the primary barrier between the NKPAF's World War 2-vintage Yak-9P fighters and UN troops fighting on the ground.

The evacuation of US citizens from Seoul via Kimpo Airport initially ran into trouble on 26 June. Enemy fighters were sighted on several occasions by F-80 pilots flying top cover over the airfield, although they obeyed orders and stayed in the vicinity of Kimpo, rather than

BELOW *Lt Charlie Wurster's F-80C FNG SPECIAL is seen at Itazuke AB during the early weeks of the war. He was flying this aircraft when he shot down a Yak-9P on 19 July 1950. The red trim indicated that the fighter was assigned to the 36th FBS. The unit temporarily traded in its jets for F-51 Mustangs shortly after this photograph was taken (Charles Wurster)*

F-80 pilots rarely returned from a mission with 0.5-in ammunition to spare, for they would diligently strafe any target they could find. With its nose supported by jacks, this 8th FBS Shooting Star is having its guns replaced at the unit's Taegu base. Note that the aircraft lacks the yellow trim synonymous with 8th FBS F-80s, indicating that it was a replacement fighter recently delivered to the unit (Budd Butcher)

ABOVE *The 'Headhunters' of the 80th FBS flew a lot of missions with their aircraft loaded in this configuration. The 1000-lb GP bomb proved most effective against deep enemy bunkers or railway marshalling yards, both of which required deep cuts to be made into the earth to have any telling effect on the enemy (Richard Durkee)*

being lured away by the Yaks. However, things got worse the following day, when NKPAF pilots decided to run the risk of being shot down in order to disrupt the evacuation effort on the ground.

Within the span of just minutes, seven communist aircraft went down in flames – four of these kills were credited to F-80 pilots from the 35th FBS, and the remaining three went to F-82 Twin Mustang crews. The Russian-built Yaks and Il-10s were no match for the F-80's speed and firepower, whilst their pilots were totally outclassed by their experienced and aggressive counterparts.

The most successful USAF pilot on this day was Lt Robert Wayne of the 35th FBS, who was the first to claim multiple victories in the same mission during the conflict. He remembers the day clearly;

'Our group (the 8th FBG) was fragged to provide cover for the C-54s that were trying to finish the evacuation from Kimpo. My flight – "C" Flight – had already logged an uneventful mission earlier that morning, and we were scheduled for another in the afternoon. During my pre-mission brief, I told my flight that when we arrived in our area, we would split into elements and set up an orbit

between the 38th Parallel to the north and Suwon to the south. We were not allowed to go north of the 38th.

'I wanted to have two aircraft heading north at all times. I don't remember the exact weather, but it couldn't have been very good – we logged one hour and forty-five minutes of weather on the mission. As I remember, the target area was something like 12,000 ft overcast, with a lower broken undercast layer at 5000 ft, with good visibility in between. Upon arriving in the target area, we split into elements and started our orbits. We had our power pulled back so that we could spend as much time as possible in the target area.

'Whilst heading north on one of our orbits, my wingman, Lt Ralph "Smiley" Hall, called out a bogey, which I could not pick up. I told him to take the lead and attack. As we turned to initiate the attack, I picked up seven prop aircraft in a loose echelon to the right. "Smiley" did not see them, so I told him to drop back on my wing. As we approached the hostile formation, I told him to line up on number seven and I lined up on number six.

'I chose these targets after spotting their loose echelon left formation, for I felt sure that all of the enemy pilots would be concentrating on the pilot just ahead and to the left of him. By adopting such a tactic we might be able to pick them off two at a time, and maybe get them all! I should mention here that during our Intelligence briefing, we were told that the British had a carrier in the Sea of Japan, and that we might see some of their aircraft in the area. Unfortunately, one of the types embarked was the Fairey Firefly V, a single-engined ground attack aircraft with a gunner in the rear cockpit – very similar in appearance to the machines that we were now tracking.

'As we closed on the formation, I saw that they matched the description of the Firefly, so I told "Smiley" to drop back until I had made a positive ID pass. As I approached the number six aircraft, I could see the rear gunner firing at me, so I told my wingman to open fire, but he was too close. I broke left and lined up behind the leading machine, firing a few rounds into it until it exploded. I then made a tight 360-degree turn to the left

and lined up behind the number two. I fired a second burst for the same results!

'By this time, I was thinking to myself that this was too easy – maybe I can get them all! I made another 360-degree turn to the left and rolled out where the number three man should have been, but the remnants of the enemy formation had all disappeared into the clouds below. I looked around the area for a few minutes, trying to find any of the remaining five, but it proved to be a futile search. Being below "bingo" fuel, I gathered up my wingman and headed back to base. The two pilots in the other element each got a kill for the day too.

'After we landed back at Itazuke, it was determined that I had fired only 328 rounds of 0.5-in ammunition.'

As Lt Wayne notes in his account, the second element in his flight also enjoyed success during this mission. Capt Schillereff and Lt Dewald were in a position

BELOW Lt Col Clure Smith, CO of the 25th FIS, poses alongside his aircraft prior to the squadron's departure from Okinawa. The 51st FIW sent two of its three squadrons to fight in the Korean War (16th and 25th FISs), while the 26th FIS remained behind to carry out the air defence of Okinawa (Frank Durkee)

ABOVE *Lt Roy Marsh shot down a North Korean Il-10 in F-80C 'LIL DOTTIE' on 29 June 1950, the 'kill' symbol for this victory being visible below the canopy rail. This photograph was taken at Suwon after the enemy had retreated back north of the 38th Parallel in the early autumn of 1950. The yellow sunburst on the fighter's vertical stabiliser was the trademark of the 80th FBS throughout the war (Roy Marsh)*

north of the leading element. Lt Robert Dewald recalls;

'Having moved away from the other element, I spotted a dark-coloured aircraft flying on a straight course south along the Naktong River. I had been listening to all the radio chatter from Bob Wayne and "Smiley" Hall, and visualising the action they were involved in.

'By the time I was able to get Capt Schillereff lined up on my wing (he had not seen the bogey yet), I found myself high above the North Korean Il-10 going in the opposite direction. I was already on my back trying to keep him in sight, pulling straight through in an almost perfect vertical curve of pursuit. As I rapidly closed, I could tell it was shaped like a fighter, but it had a cockpit that seemed to be long enough to have a second crewman behind the pilot.

'Suddenly, I noticed what seemed like a blinking light in the rear cockpit, and realised that there was a gunner behind a gun and he was firing at me! I was converging

fast and was well within range, so I pulled off a long burst with all six "fifties", firing into the Il-10's cockpit area. The pilot took no evasive action, flying straight and level, so I pulled up and positioned myself for another firing pass.

'This time there was no light blinking from the rear gun, so I put another long burst into the fuselage and walked it on up to the engine. Again, there were no apparent results – no smoke – and the prop was still turning, keeping the aircraft in straight and level flight. This called for me to line up for a third pass, so I dropped far enough back to allow me to level off and come up behind at point blank range.

'I made a long firing pass, and still there was no evidence of any damage to the Il-10, but I noticed that his angle of descent had increased quite dramatically. Having pulled in closely behind the aircraft in order to ascertain its condition, I suddenly found my windscreen covered with engine oil – glancing off to each side, I saw that the

BELOW
RAMBLIN=RECK=TEW *was the personal mount of Lt Robert Dewald of the 35th FBS. On 27 June 1950, he shot down a North Korean Il-10 over the Seoul area whilst at the controls of this machine – the jet's 'kill' symbol has again been applied below the canopy rail. The 35th FBS scored four kills in just a matter of minutes on this day, making it the first F-80 outfit to be credited with aerial victories (Robert Dewald)*

ABOVE The 'office' for Shooting Star pilots during the Korean War. This photograph reveals the left console of a 16th FIS F-80C at Suwon AB in early 1951 (Carl Ebneter)

same oil had covered my leading edges and tip tanks! Low on fuel, my wingman and I climbed for altitude and rode some good tailwinds back to Itazuke. After our gun camera film was analysed, it was determined that we had each downed an Il-10 apiece. My victory had been earned the hard way!'

F-80 squadrons continued to fly these top cover missions for the next few days, pilots heading up to the Kimpo/Seoul area to await the arrival of the NKPAF. On 30 June, the North Koreans again ventured south in force, and this time two Yak-9Ps fell to the guns of the F-80. 36th FBS pilot Lt Charles Wurster, flying his assigned jet FNG SPECIAL, claimed one of the kills;

'My wingman and I were somewhere in the vicinity of Suwon when we were jumped by two aggressive Yak-9 types. For a few moments we were at a disadvantage, as we had been caught at low altitude. However, the superior acceleration of the F-80 soon gave us the advantage over the Yaks. It was over in a few seconds, as I came in fast from the North Korean's rear.

'My closure was so fast that I don't know if he even saw me. I let go with a long burst, walking it all over his fuselage, wing root and vertical stabiliser. Immediately, the Yak was out of control, and the pilot successfully bailed out. We later surmised that both of the pilots must have been instructor types, for they were much better than those we had been encountering.'

More kills were accrued in July, and by the 20th of that month, F-80 pilots had been credited with a total of 14 confirmed air-to-air kills over North Korean aircraft. The war was less than 30 days old, yet UN intelligence reports were stating that the NKPAF had all but ceased to exist. The communists still had a significant number of flyable aircraft, but they had fled en masse across the border into Manchuria, where they were scattered over several airfields.

Now fitted with new 'Misawa' tip tanks, F-80s were roaming all over North Korea by August. Bombing all manner of targets, pilots also very occasionally surprised enemy aircraft found hiding at the few battered airfields

that remained operational along the Yalu. Usually flown in at dusk, these aircraft were located at first light by RF-80s conducting their daily photo-runs.

A strike mission would be immediately generated, resulting in the fighter-bombers heading north on yet another 'hunting trip' — records show that approximately 24 aircraft were destroyed on the ground by marauding F-80s in the three-month period July to September 1950.

The first sightings of Russian-built MiG-15s south of the Yalu River in early November changed the freedom with which the F-80s overflew North Korea. The first knowledge the USAF had of the existence of the superlative communist fighter came via blurred imagery caught on F-51 gun camera film. The MiG-15 posed a definite threat to the UN's continued air supremacy in-theatre, so the decision was made to post the F-86A Sabre-equipped 4th FIW to Korea.

The plan was for the very latest USAF jet fighter to counter its Soviet counterpart, while F-80s and F-51s continued to pound targets on the ground. However, the

Sabres would not arrive in Korea until mid-December, and it became inevitable that the Shooting Stars would clash with MiG-15s well before this. And so on 8 November 1950, the world's first jet-versus-jet engagement was fought out.

On this day, four Shooting Stars from the 16th FIS were sent on a bombing mission against anti-aircraft batteries around the airfield at Sinuiju. The senior pilot in the flight was the 16th's commanding officer, Lt Col Evans G Stephens, and on his wing was 1Lt Russell J Brown. The latter pilot was on his first mission 'up on the river' (he was on temporary duty with the 16th FIS from the Okinawa-based 26th FIS), and it was his element that felt the brunt of the attack from the MiG-15s.

The following account of this historic engagement draws on the experiences of both Lt Col Stephens and Lt Brown. The unit CO remembers;

'After we had successfully delivered our bombs on target, we took up a heading to the south-east in a low angle climb to gain distance and altitude. As flight leader, I

ABOVE *Same cockpit, different view. This time, the photographer (16th FIS pilot Lt Carl Ebneter) has focused on the instrument panel and gunsight (Carl Ebneter)*

RIGHT *Four 51st FIW F-80 pilots pose for the camera at Kimpo AB in the autumn of 1950. Second from the right is 1Lt Russell J Brown, who made history when he became the first USAF jet pilot to shoot down a MiG-15 in a highly publicised engagement fought over North Korea on 8 November 1950. A 26th FIS pilot, Brown was TDY with the 16th FIS when he scored his MiG kill (Dick Escola)*

used 97 per cent power so as to allow the rest of my flight to join up after their strafing passes.

'At this time, there was some radio chatter from another flight that stated there were numerous aircraft in the air coming south across the river – I started a shallow turn to the left for a better view in that direction. I would guess that we were about four miles south of the Yalu, and the number three and four aircraft in my flight were about a quarter-mile behind us. Lt Brown, my wingman, was about 100 yards away at my four o'clock.'

Lt Brown vividly remembers that when Lt Col Stephens called out that there were eight MiGs north of the river, they were showing no sign of turning to the south;

'As a matter of fact, they were doing loops and barrel rolls! I thought to myself that this has got to be a crazy war when the enemy can practice stunt flying right in front of you! Suddenly, all hell broke loose. Lt Col Stephens shouted for me to break left. An instant later two flashing silver aircraft dove at me out of the sun. As they swept by, I opened the throttle and tacked onto the tail of one of them, trying to manoeuvre into a firing position. These were definitely MiGs, and I got a clear look at the communist jet as it started to climb back up into

the sun. The aircraft had no distinguishing markings – just polished aluminium, swept wings and plenty fast!'

Lt Col Stephens continues;

'As the lead MiG passed me, I could see a red star on the side of the fuselage. By the time I could get a good pursuit curve on the lead, he was at least 1500 ft out, and moving away. I held a long burst on him and saw some debris come off of his left wing. At that time, he turned sharply and headed for the safety of the Yalu.'

In the meantime, Lt Brown, ahead of Stephens in the fracas, adds more narrative;

'When the MiG ahead of me broke to the left, he made a fatal mistake. He could climb faster than I could, but when he turned, I cut him off and got in four good short bursts with my guns. It was difficult to tell if I had hit him. He just rolled over and headed for the deck in a steep dive. I racked my F-80 around and followed him down. My airspeed was indicating over 600 mph, but I could not close the gap!

'At this time, he was about 1000 ft away when I gave him another four bursts. Black smoke spouted from the right side of his fuselage. I knew it was now or never, so I squeezed off one long burst. Orange flames licked back over his fuselage and, suddenly, the entire MiG exploded

BELOW *Head down in the cockpit, an 80th FBS pilot makes his final cockpit checks prior to taxiing out on a close support mission. His jet is armed with just four 5-in HVARs and 0.5-in ammunition due to the fact that he is flying from Itazuke, rather than a base in Korea. This shot was taken in early 1951, when UN ground forces were still trying to stall the first Chinese offensive into South Korea (Chuck Baisden)*

in mid-air! After that I don't remember what happened, as I was too busy trying to pull out of my high speed dive.'

Lt Col Stephens fills in the final moments;

'About the time that Lt Brown began his high angle diving pursuit of the MiG, I rolled left to see an F-80 about 3000 ft below me in a dive. I then looked for the rest of my flight, and to see if any other MiGs were in the area – especially if one was on my tail. Looking back, I saw the F-80 starting to pull out of its dive, and I saw the impact explosion of the MiG as it hit the ground.

'At the onset of the fight, I did not call for the lead element to drop tanks because it would have put them into the path of numbers three and four trailing behind us. Lt Brown did not realise that the high speed pull-up caused wing "twist" due to his tanks still being attached.'

This all-jet dogfight had lasted only a minute, yet it created a sensation with the US press corps in-theatre. And unknown to everyone at the time, it was only a portent of things to come! The MiG-15 pilots continued to grow in confidence, fully aware that their most dangerous adversaries then in-theatre were flying inferior straight-winged F-80s and F9F Panthers.

Soon after this initial MiG kill, 25th FIS CO, Lt Col Clure Smith, found himself leading a flight of F-80s on an escort mission for fighter-bombers over the Yalu;

'I was leading a flight of four over the river when I spotted four MiGs taking off from Antung. I watched them climb out and turn to the south. When they were definitely south of the Yalu, I called for my flight to jettison tanks and we dove down on them. Seconds later, they saw us, and they triggered their external tanks too, with the exception of the leader. His hung up, so he was the one I went after. With his tanks hanging on, the MiG pilot had no advantage over my F-80.

'I scored hits all over his fuselage and he dove back toward the safety of the river. There was never any confirmation as to whether he made it back to base, but the time frame was about when Lt Brown got his MiG-15.'

In an article that appeared in the *Stars and Stripes* on 15 December 1950, statistics were given to chart the rise of UN of air power during the first six months of the war;

'Until the step up of MiG-15 activity in November, there was almost no comparison between United Nations and communist air activity. From June 25th through December 8th, only 506 sorties were known to have been flown by the communists. During this same time period, the American Far Eastern Air Force flew approximately 72,000 sorties. This did not count all of those flown by Navy and Marine aircraft. If this had been factored in, the total would have been well over 100,000 sorties.'

These figures had been released to *Stars and Stripes* by HQ FEAF.

OPPOSITE *Getting jumped by MiG-15s whilst coming off a bomb run was commonplace for UN fighter-bomber pilots. This F-80 caught two 37 mm cannon rounds in its rear fuselage section, yet it still made it back to base. Had the shells struck home just a few feet forward or aft, they could have proven fatal to both the aircraft and its pilot (who was flying his 98th mission when this occurred). Scores of F-80s made it back to their bases with gaping holes in the wings and fuselage, proving the strength of the Lockheed fighter-bomber (Richard Hellwege)*

There is no doubt that the 16th FIS's SARA SUE was not looking her best when this shot was taken! Resting on empty fuel drums in the bone yard at Suwon, the jet had returned to base with flak damage, which had in turn caused its undercarriage to collapse on landing. Never to fly again, a significant portion of the aircraft has been stripped of parts in order to keep other F-80s airworthy (John Nossick)

INSET LEFT *While its two sister squadrons were deployed to South Korea, the 26th FIS stayed behind to perform the air defence role for the Okinawa Sector. However, most of the unit's pilots saw action whilst on TDY with either the 16th or 25th FISs. This yellow-trimmed 26th F-80 is seen here on the alert pad at Naha AB in 1950 (Dick Escola)*

INSET RIGHT *The business end of an F-80C is clearly shown in this unusual view. The six M-3 0.5-in (12.7 mm) machine guns concentrated in the nose of the Shooting Star could fire a significant number of rounds into a very concentrated area, giving the jet superior killing power. This was probably the last view a rear gunner in an Il-10 had prior to his mount being shot out of the sky. This particular F-80 was flown by the 'Head Hunters' of the 80th FBS (Richard Durkee)*

MAIN PICTURE *Thrust aloft partially by the boost provided by its JATO bottles, this 7th FBS F-80C is seen departing Taegu at the start of a major strike against Sinuiju in May 1951. Several weeks later the unit traded in its war-weary F-80s for new F-84 Thunderjets. All of the Shooting Stars visible here were assigned to the 49th FBW (George Rutter)*

RIGHT *This photograph was taken at Suwon in October 1950, and it shows 80th FBS pilots loading up for the ride out to the flightline for yet another mission against the retreating NKPA. F-80 squadrons kept the maximum number of aircraft bombed up and in the air during this period. These men would probably have had to fly north of Pyongyang to locate good targets (Don Loegering)*

LEFT *Anti-aircraft fire around any of North Korea's high priority assets was always extremely heavy. Indeed, most F-80s would return to base with some degree of battle damage following a mission 'up north'. Having suffered numerous hits while pulling out of a dive-bombing run, the pilot of this 35th FBS 'Black Panthers' F-80 experienced total hydraulic failure on landing at Taegu. The jet eventually skidded to a halt on its belly off the side of the runway (H P Saabye)*

BELOW LEFT *The wear and tear on jet engines was phenomenal in Korea. Indeed, engine changes became so routine that they could be performed in virtually any weather, and in virtually any location. If such heavy maintenance could not have been undertaken at forward bases, the in-service rate for the F-80 would have been unacceptably low. In turn, the pressure applied by fighter-bombers on the enemy's supply lines would have been significantly reduced. This engine change was photographed well underway at Taegu in the early autumn of 1950. The black panther painted just below the jet's cockpit indicated that it was assigned to the 35th FBS (Frederic Champlin)*

CHAPTER THREE
F-80s VERSUS THE 'MIGHTY DRAGON'

BELOW *The F-80 was rarely seen bombed up in this configuration due to the jet's notoriously short range. However, when performing missions close to the frontline – officially titled the Main Line of Resistance (MLR) – that had a flying time of less than one hour, the F-80 was cleared to operate with its tip tanks replaced by two 1000-lb bombs. Boasting a warload of 4000 lbs, this combination proved most effective against deep enemy bunkers and ammunition dumps located immediately behind the frontline. This particular aircraft was assigned to the 36th FBS at Suwon (K-13) (Richard Durkee)*

UN forces experienced the highs and lows of war during the course of November 1950. Having pushed the NKPA back north across the 38th Parallel, and succeeded in driving on to Pyongyang, the battle-weary troops were expecting the Korean War to be over by Christmas. However, on 26 November the Chinese Army powered its way into North Korea, leaving UN forces with little choice but to retreat in the face of overwhelming communist numerical superiority.

The warning signs that the Chinese were moving a substantial number of troops across the frozen Yalu in preparation for the surprise invasion had been totally ignored by the UN commander-in-theatre, Gen Douglas MacArthur, and his staff. Moving under the cover of darkness, Chinese troops had been regularly detected by patrolling B-26 crews (see *Osprey Frontline Colour 4 - B-26 Invader Units over Korea* for further details), as well as

Marine nightfighter pilots who were hunting out communist trucks travelling on the main supply route between Manchuria and Sinuiju.

MacArthur's intelligence picture was based almost exclusively on photographs generated by daylight reconnaissance flights performed by RF-80s. These missions were flown to a rigid schedule, and the Chinese quickly figured out when the jets were due and simply camouflaged their invasion preparations accordingly.

With the NKPAF having 'gone silent' in late August, the F-80 units in-theatre abandoned the air superiority mission and flew myriad interdiction and close air support sorties. During September and October, the jets delivered just about every type of ordnance against targets across the length and breadth of North Korea.

Controlling the skies, the UN seemed to have an equally strong grip on the ground war too, although this

was all set to change on the night of 26 November, when Chinese infantry attacked a Republic of Korea Army unit. The firepower directed at the Korean troops soon ensured a breakthrough in the UN frontline, and within hours the communist offensive was in full swing. At first, there was total disbelief within Gen MacArthur's HQ that such an attack could have been launched, but on the morning of the 27th stark reality set in, for UN positions were being overrun by a truly massive Chinese force.

At this point in the war, all six F-80 squadrons in-theatre were operating from Korean soil. This meant that they could give better aerial support for troops on the ground, and they were quickly called into action.

26th FIS pilot Lt Dick Escola was on TDY with the 16th FIS in November 1950, and he was also in the air at the time the first jet-versus-jet engagement took place close to the Chinese border;

'On 8 November we briefed for a strike mission against the airfield at Sinuiju, our jets being loaded with 5-in rockets. We performed the rocket runs in very loose trail, so that our rockets wouldn't catch up to the guy flying in front. All that I saw on the ground were revetments, which I fired on. When we had used all of our HVARs, we climbed up to 20,000 ft to rendezvous with the remaining flights, and to act as their fighter cover whilst they delivered their ordnance.

'Before we had time to join up, someone called out "MiGs", and we anxiously scoured the sky in an effort to locate them. As I looked to the right, I spotted a MiG descending across my flightpath at high speed. Being well below bore-sight speed, I tried to figure out where my bullets would actually go. I aimed in the general area that my gunsight displayed, "walked" the rudders a little to make up for not knowing just where to aim, and fired – I evidently didn't guess right, because I failed to see any hits on the MiG.

'It was at about this time that Lt Russell Brown said he was firing at a MiG in an almost vertical dive. He said his aircraft was buffeting quite a bit because he was exceeding .80 mach. Seconds later, Brown had a confirmed kill. What started out as a regular air-to-ground strike had turned out to be one of the "big events" of the whole war.'

At this stage of the conflict, F-80 pilots typically flew one of four types of mission, as Lt George R Veazey of the 36th FBS explains;

'The usual mission was "pre-briefed", with a flight of four briefed to attack a specific target. A second type was a "JOC" (Joint Operations Command) mission, usually flown by a flight of four who had been on alert. They would be sent to attack a target called in by a frontline observer or a reconnaissance aircraft. A third type was a

BELOW *Three 'Head Hunters' from the 80th FBS taxi onto the main runway at Suwon prior to launching on a short-range mission against Chinese troop concentrations close to the frontline. Each F-80 is loaded with napalm, which proved to be the most feared, and effective, weapon against communist ground forces. This photograph was taken in late 1951 after the 8th FBG had moved all three of its squadrons to Suwon. The group would remain at this base until war's end (Chuck Baisden)*

RIGHT *When Chinese forces pushed UN troops back south of the 38th Parallel, F-80 units were forced to flee Korean soil and return to bases in Japan – such as Tsuiki, where this photograph was taken in May 1951. The yellow trim on the jet in the foreground indicates an 8th FBS machine, whilst the F-80C with blue unit markings belongs to the 7th FBS. Both squadrons were part of the 49th FBG, which was in the process of converting from F-80s to brand new F-84 Thunderjets. The group would operate the Republic fighter-bomber until war's end (George Rutter)*

pre-briefed mission flown in squadron strength (12 aircraft) or, on rare occasions, group strength (48 aircraft). The fourth type was a "late light recce", where the flight of four would take off just before dusk and bomb a road with a partial load to make a cut, then fly north for 15 minutes or so before returning to bomb and strafe trucks that were backed up at the freshly-made road cut.

'A very experienced pilot – an "old head" – usually flew lead on the four-ship missions, and after each and every sortie missions there was a debriefing of each flight member by Intelligence personnel.'

Much of North Korea is covered in mountainous terrain, criss-crossed with valleys. The communists would take advantage of this terrain by constructing truck and train routes through the valleys, and these proved to be irresistible targets for F-80 pilots. However, attacking trucks and trains in these areas was a risky business, particularly once the Chinese began surrounding the routes with gun emplacements.

These missions had been dangerous from the early weeks of the war, however, for the NKPA had adopted the practice of stringing cables across the valleys to catch unsuspecting fighter-bombers. Indeed, one of the first aircraft lost during the war was an F-82 Twin Mustang that flew into one of these cables – a large number of night-marauding B-26s were also downed this way.

Here, Lt Charles Wurster of the 36th FBS relates an experience he had with a cable on a low-level mission;

'I was stacked up on my element leader, Lt Ellis, on a low-level close air support sortie over the frontlines. I was busy watching Ellis's aeroplane, but out of the corner of my eye I saw a black line coming at me. I popped the stick and heard a loud thud. Glancing up into my rear view mirror, I didn't see anything – not even my vertical stabiliser. I knew I had hit a cable, and my immediate reaction was to pull up and head south.

'I made it up to 30,000 ft, attempting to make radio contact with Ellis whilst gaining height. My antennae had also been sheared off, however, so naturally there was no response to my calls. When I got to the coast above Pusan, I had to make a decision whether to try to land there, or fly back across the Sea of Japan to Itazuke. With my aircraft still handling, I chose to return home, landing back at base without any great problems. Needless to say, I created a lot of attention when I touched down with no tail. Had I been flying a few feet higher, or in a slight bank, when I made contact with the cable, it could have been disastrous.'

The ultimate goal of all fighter interceptor pilots was to 'bag' at least one MiG-15, and if you were lucky enough, get five and become an ace. Fighter-bomber pilots had very little opportunity to score aerial kills once the

LEFT *Weighed down with napalm and fully laden 'Misawa' tip tanks, this 7th FBS F-80 has had to resort to using JATO bottles to help it get airborne from Tsuiki. This unit regularly flew escort missions for RF-80s in early December 1950, the F-80s eventually being replaced in this hazardous mission by F-86s. Shooting Star pilots scrapped with their communist counterparts in MiG-15s on several occasions during this period, although neither side could claim any victories (George Rutter)*

BELOW LEFT *It would have been hard to have missed the Combat Operations Center for the 8th FBG at Suwon. All three of the group's colourful squadrons were represented on this sign, their lineage going all the way back to the 1930s. The group spent the first weeks of World War 2 in the Pacific, although from 1942 through to the present day, the 8th has been associated with the Far East. The group presently flies F-16 Fighting Falcons out of Kunsan, in South Korea, and has been known as the 'Wolf Pack' since its Vietnam War days, when it flew the F-4 Phantom II (Robert Crackel)*

frontline settled down into stalemate in 1951. Instead of MiGs, 'mud moving' types hoped to catch a train out in the open and take out the engine. Unfortunately, these targets also became more and more scarce as the war progressed, with trains usually running only at night.

The nightflying B-26s were the high scorers when it came to knocking out locomotives, although F-80 pilots were willing to take great risks to get down low enough to skip bomb the tunnels that they often hid in during the day. They became very successful at this tactic, the intricacies of which are explained here by 8th FBS 'Black Sheep' pilot, Lt Budd Butcher;

'Train-busting was our favourite interdiction mission! Not only did it do considerable damage to the communist war effort, it was downright fun to "blow up an engine", stop the train and then work over the rail cars, which were normally full of supplies and munitions. At times, the secondary explosions were extremely spectacular. However, train-busting was not without great risk to a pilot's well being!

'Flak guns were always placed at various locations along the train. Within seconds of coming under attack, the sides of some cars would drop down, giving the anti-aircraft gunners an unobstructed field of fire.

'In March 1951, I led a flight of three F-80Cs on a dawn (first light) armed reconnaissance patrol in search of targets of opportunity. Supply trains were at the top of our priority list! Arriving in the target area just as the sun came up was critical, for it was the only way to catch trains before they hid in the tunnels for the day.

'I spotted a long freight (ammo supply) train near Sonchon, its driver going as fast as he could in an effort to make it to a nearby tunnel. He didn't make it! I managed to blow the engine on the first pass, stopping his forward progress. It amazed me what six 0.5-in guns could do! As soon as this happened, the train's entire complement of anti-aircraft guns opened up on us, making the task all the more interesting. The three of us worked over the rail cars until our ammo was exhausted.

'We got quite a few spectacular secondary explosions from the cars, as well as neutralising the AA guns. I called for more flights to come in and finish off the train. It was a very rewarding mission, which earned me my first DFC.'

It was rare for fighter-bombers to catch a train moving after first light, so pilots had to become proficient at skip-bombing a 500-lb device, fitted with a delayed-action fuse, into a train tunnel. This proved to be a lot harder than it looked, for the tunnels were obviously located in mountainous terrain, which made them difficult to approach at the appropriate angle for bomb release.

36th FBS pilot Lt Gene Crackel skip-bombed, although he can't vouch for the results of his attack;

OPPOSITE *Lt Col Ben Warren, CO of the 16th FIS, takes time out to have his picture taken with one of his squadron's F-80Cs. Behind him, the maintenance crews are busy getting the battle-weary jet ready for yet another mission from of Suwon in 1951. The squadron would give up its Shooting Stars in late November 1951, the Lockheed fighters being replaced by new F-86Es. As part of the 51st FIW, the 16th FIS had become one of the USAF's leading MiG killing squadrons by war's end (Bill Williams)*

'Intelligence reported that a train had pulled into a railroad tunnel, so two flights of F-80s were despatched to destroy it. We circled over the target area, with each pilot taking it in turns to break away and make a low-level skip-bombing run against the hidden locomotive. The bombs were fitted with delayed-action fuses so that we wouldn't blow ourselves up when they hit the ground.

'I recall seeing several pilots make their runs, causing puffs of dust to kick up as the bombs skipped across the ground at the mouth of the tunnel. They all missed. When I made my run, I discovered it wasn't easy. The valley was narrower and more crooked than it appeared from above – I had to zig and zag at about 400 mph. I released my two bombs and they were never heard from again! No one saw them hit outside the tunnel, so they must have gone in. But, there was no evidence of any explosions – no dust and no debris coming from either end of the tunnel. We never knew what happened, but if they had exploded, I think it would have collapsed the tunnel and destroyed the train!'

On several occasions, missions were flown against these tunnels with bigger 1000-lb bombs. Lt Jerry Minton

of the 80th FBS participated in at least one of these missions;

'I can remember a few of the unusual missions we flew, and one in particular where we flew down a railroad track, one at a time, attempting to skip 1000-lb bombs into two rail tunnels that went through a hill. One pilot in our flight put one in each tunnel on his pass, while the rest of us bounced and blew bombs everywhere. I don't know if we used any more of the big bombs on this type of mission.

'On most of our missions, our bombs were usually set at three-second delay, which allowed penetration after impact. However, on certain types of targets such as bridges, rail lines and some airfields, the delay fuses were set as far out as 72 hours. This was done in an effort to sap the repair crew's enthusiasm and morale when it came to rectifying bomb damage.'

Although the Shooting Star's arsenal of weaponry remained virtually unchanged throughout the war, occasionally the delivery of these bombs, rockets and napalm would be altered in order to counter a new enemy threat.

BELOW *Lt Charles Wurster and his crew chief take a look at the missing vertical stabiliser on his 36th FBS F-80. The pilot had hit a cable that had been strung across a valley, and despite this damage, he was able to bring the aircraft safely back to Itazuke AB. His account of this incident is featured on page 56 (Charles Wurster)*

For example, when the NKPAF began flying nocturnal harassment missions with the Po-2 biplane, an immediate effort was made by the fighter-bomber pilots to negate this new threat by bombing. The F-80 squadrons bombed some of the lesser known grass strips in North Korea, which were deemed suitable for these aircraft to operate from. Lt George R Veazey remembers flying a few of these sorties;

'On some special missions we carried four 1000-lb bombs and no tip tanks. These were usually against crude grass fields that could be used by "Bed Check Charlie's" bi-wing Po-2s. They were constantly harassing our major bases by flying over at night and dropping grenades or small bombs. Our bombs on these missions were equipped with a combination of instant and time-delay fuses – some of the delays were up to 12 hours or more. The airfields were rendered inoperable by our attacks, and aircraft could only use them again after urgent repair work had been carried out. And this became a dangerous proposition thanks to the delayed-action fuses.'

It was a known fact that the communists could only get labourers back on the job by threatening them with execution after so many of their comrades had been killed by late-detonating bombs.

Flying so many sorties every single day, it was inevitable that occasionally the aim of the F-80 pilots would be a little off. Indeed, anyone could have a bad day, and with anti-aircraft fire literally surrounding you on virtually every mission, it took nerves of steel to stay focused on the bombsight as the target loomed large. Many bombs that drifted off course and blew up harmlessly were put down to the inexperience, or momentary ineptitude, of the pilot.

35th FBS pilot Lt Ed Skaggs recalls one mission where the bombs caused more damage by actually missing the designated target;

'We were on the way to T-Bone Ridge for a close support mission. It was being co-ordinated by one of the T-6 Mosquito pilots. Before we hit the target area, my radio went out, so I signalled my number three slot to take over.

'The Mosquito pilot marked the target with smoke rockets as the new flight leader rolled in on the markers. The balance of our flight orbited to see what the lead

would do (if he took out the target, then we would divert to secondary targets in the area). Number three's bombs hit about 150 metres from the marker, so we lined up to make our runs, but before we could roll over and head down, there was a tremendous secondary explosion! Lead had accidentally hit a hidden ammunition dump, and Chinese soldiers were scattering all over the place. The balance of the flight went in and expended its ordnance, shooting up everything in sight. We did a lot of damage on that mission!'

The Chinese were generally more interested in protecting their supply routes to the front than their troops. The primary reason for this was that most troops within close proximity of the frontlines were dug in so deep that it would have been difficult for the fighter-bombers to have inflicted any serious losses. However, the key rail lines, road junctions and tunnels were vulnerable to attack, and therefore had to be protected.

This meant that each of these targets was surrounded by anti-aircraft artillery and numerous automatic weapons. The density of these increased significantly in early 1952, thus heightening the risk posed to the fighter-bombers tasked with attacking these key targets. New approach tactics were quickly devised to increase the chances of mission survivability, these being adopted by F-51, F-80 and F-84 units.

The new procedures called for the aircraft to enter the target area through the sector that offered the least resistance in terms of flak. Pilots then made a 90-degree turn towards the target flight by flight, releasing their

OPPOSITE TOP *This flightline shot of 8th FBS F-80s clearly shows the large number of replacement aircraft that were required to keep a frontline unit at full strength. Indeed, only one aircraft appears to have the unit's distinctive yellow markings and emblem. This photograph was taken in February 1951 at Taegu, when UN troops were still trying to check the Chinese offensive (Budd Butcher)*

LEFT *This 8th FBS machine is undergoing a 100-hour inspection in the open at Taegu in the early winter of 1950 – temperatures had already dropped below freezing at night. In the months that followed, the 'Black Sheep' became well versed in the art of locomotive hunting during 'first light' missions (Budd Butcher)*

ABOVE *The F-80 proved itself to be every bit as rugged as its piston-engined forebears from World War 2, being able to absorb heavy battle damage of the sort shown in this photograph. This 80th FBS fighter-bomber hit a cable while on a low-level strafing run through a mountain valley in North Korea – the pilot was still able to land the F-80 back at Suwon. The enemy's use of cables was an on-going problem for the duration of the war (Chuck Baisden)*

bombs at a relatively high altitude (approximately 6000 ft) in order to allow them to immediately recover from their dive and instigate a sharp breakaway from the target area!

With formations of 12 or more aircraft, the first flight carried V/T (proximity-fused) bombs for flak suppression. These would explode above-ground, causing maximum casualties amongst flak crews. When attacking in smaller numbers, only the first two aircraft carried this type of ordnance.

The enemy soon became aware of these tactics, and the first few aircraft were allowed through to the target without opposition, while the latter elements caught the full brunt of the flak defences. F-80 pilots countered this move by placing their V/T bombs in the middle of the formation, allowing the first aircraft to do significant damage with their regular 500-lb GP bombs.

Aside from myriad ground attack missions, F-80 units still occasionally flew fighter sweeps during the early months of 1951. Of course the 4th FIW was the primary fighter unit in-theatre, but its F-86s were spread very thinly at this time, for there was not available space in Korea to support all three squadrons. This meant that at least one unit had to remain back in Japan at all times.

The Sabre wing did its best to take on the MiGs, whilst still maintaining a protective umbrella over the large formations of fighter-bombers that were flying up into 'MiG Alley' on a daily basis. This often left B-29 formations tasked with performing strategic bombing raids against industrial targets deep within North Korea without dedicated fighter cover.

Reverting to one of their pre-war missions, F-80 units stepped into the breach to fly bomber escort, although

they proved only marginally successful in this role due to the jet's excessive fuel consumption. By the time pilots had set up a defensive screen above the bombers, their F-80s were already running low on fuel, and should the bombers be running behind schedule, then the fighters would have to head back to base before the B-29s had even arrived at the rendezvous point.

The worst example of this occurred in early March 1951 when 18 B-29s ran into a headwind. By the time they reached the target area, 22 F-80s had already been forced to head home. Left with just a handful of covering fighters, the bombers were set upon by nine MiG-15s, which succeeded in badly damaging ten of them. Indeed, three were in such poor shape that they crash-landed at bases in Korea. Not long after this, B-29s switched to night operations, which did not require fighter escorts.

Despite its obvious shortcomings as a fighter, the F-80 proved itself over and over again in the ground attack role. And it was fitting that the type's sole Medal of Honor winner (one of only four such decorations presented to members of the USAF in Korea) earned his award flying in support of 'grunts on the ground'. On 22 November 1952, 80th FBS flight leader Maj Charles J Loring Jr led his section against gun emplacements which were firing on UN troops dug in nearby.

The major's F-80 suffered several hits during one of his dive-bombing runs, making it impossible for him to return to base. Wrestling with the controls of his stricken jet, Loring succeeded in gaining sufficient altitude to allow him to dive at the enemy guns one last time. He crashed his F-80 squarely into the emplacement, resulting in a violent explosion which instantly killed Maj Loring.

ABOVE *A mixed team of USAF and South Korean personnel were responsible for delivering bombs to the flightline at Suwon AB. These 1000-lb GP bombs are destined for 35th FBS F-80Cs tasked with fulfilling the day's mission requirements. Note the well maintained PSP and the sandbagged revetments – both features designed to protect aircraft from the possibility of attacks by night-flying Po-2s. They also helped facilitate smooth operations in damp winter weather (Richard Durkee)*

8th FBS 'Black Sheep' pilots pose for the camera prior to climbing into their respective cockpits at the start of another mission. With most sorties that were flown being performed by flights of four aircraft, most informal group shots consisted of a quartet of pilots – the individual on the extreme left is Lt Budd Butcher. Quite a few of the pilots who served with this unit had spent time as forward air controllers with troops in the frontline, giving them a greater appreciation of how best to support fighting men on the ground. The unit's F-80s were well known for their bright yellow trim and squadron emblem painted on either side of the fuselage (Budd Butcher)

These four 'Headhunters' from the 80th FBS are suited up ready to fly. Their unit flew F-80s in combat longer than any other squadron, being one of the first fighter-bomber outfits thrust into action in June 1950. The 80th would continue to operate Shooting Stars until late April 1953, when it finally transitioned to the new F-86F fighter-bomber (Charles Rowan)

ABOVE *A rare shot of a 9th FBS F-80 'on the wing' returning to Taegu after a bombing mission north of the 38th Parallel – FT-811 was regularly flown by Lt John S Starck. The 9th was one of three squadrons under the command of the 49th FBG. In 1951, this group would turn all of its F-80s over to the 8th FBG following its transition onto the F-84 (Richard Immig)*

RIGHT *This 8th FBS F-80C is undergoing minor maintenance out in the open at Taegu AB in May 1951 – just prior to the squadron receiving its first F-84s. The aircraft has been sat on jacks, which would indicate that it may be suffering from landing gear problems (Budd Butcher)*

LEFT *A large number of South Korean labourers were trained to work with the USAF's armourers in the bomb dumps. They would usually be employed hauling bombs from the assembly area to the flightline, and a few were even allowed to load the ordnance onto aircraft – they were always closely supervised in the latter role, however. Hundreds of civilian types could be found performing all manner of menial tasks on bases across South Korea throughout the war. This group are seen on the 35th FBS's flightline at Suwon AB (Harvey Weaver)*

These four 35th FBS pilots have finished their mission briefing and are ready to strap in to their jets for a bombing sortie against Chinese targets above the MLR. The squadron was known as the 'Black Panthers', and all of its aircraft carried the blue sunburst on their vertical stabilisers. The 35th was the highest-scoring F-80 squadron in terms of aerial kills, with its pilots downing seven NKPAF machines in the first four weeks of the war (Richard Durkee)

INSET *8th FBS pilot 1Lt James R Markette poses on the flightline at Taegu AB in full flying gear in front of his jet, which is in the process of being made ready for its next mission. Note the 49th FBG emblem painted on the nose access panel (James Markette)*

MAIN PICTURE *An ample supply of napalm and bombs have been brought up from the bomb dump and positioned next to the flightline of the 36th FBS. This photograph was taken in late 1951, when the 8th FBG was launching as many aircraft as it could on a daily basis. Although the Chinese advance had been checked some months earlier, the communists kept on bringing in enormous amounts of supplies in preparation for another offensive. The ordnance shown here would have been used up in less than a day (Ken Rowntree)*

ABOVE The South Korean Air Force Academy, located at Chinhae, produced some excellent fighter pilots. Always keen to view frontline operations at first hand, cadets were constantly visiting the various bases throughout South Korea. These students were photographed on the 7th FBS's flightline at Taegu (James McKendry)

RIGHT Dawn at Suwon. These 35th FBS F-80s have already been loaded with napalm, the groundcrews having prepped each aircraft prior to the arrival of the pilots from their early-morning mission briefing (Russ Rogers)

LEFT *Lt Clarence 'Klu' Hoggard stands on the ladder leading up to the cockpit of his F-80. A 100-mission veteran of the 36th FBS, he would remain in the USAF post-war and eventually see more combat in F-105s during the Vietnam War (Clarence Hoggard)*

ABOVE This rare shot of a 41st FIS Shooting Star was taken at Taegu AB (K-2). It was apparently flown in as a replacement aircraft for the 49th FBG, as the 41st was strictly an air defence unit based at Johnson AB, in Japan (Nat King)

RIGHT Both of the USAF's high profile fighter-bombers (the F-80 and F-84) went after bridges in North Korea in a big way, with units quickly finding that the 1000-lb GP bomb was the most effective against these targets. The centre span of this bridge had been knocked out by fighter-bombers early in the war, and the communists had made no effort to repair it prior to its recapture by UN forces (Evans Stephens)

LEFT *Taking a moment to relax for the camera, Lt Jack Broughton leans against the wing of his 8th FBS F-80C at Taegu. His target for the next mission would require 5-in rockets and napalm, which have already been loaded beneath the wings of his aircraft. Broughton would later become one of the most respected F-105 pilots to see action in the Vietnam War, writing the acclaimed autobiographical volumes* Thud Ridge *and* Going Downtown
(Jack Broughton)

CHAPTER FOUR

FROM DAWN TO DUSK

Once the 'human waves' of Chinese troops had been stopped and the frontline began to stabilise somewhere around the 38th Parallel, little changed in terms of territorial gains for either side from the summer of 1951 through to the end of the Korean War in July 1953. Yet despite each day seeing the same missions flown by the fighter-bomber units, the degree of danger associated with these sorties had increased dramatically.

Due to overwhelming air power exerted in-theatre by the UN air forces, the enemy had been forced to camouflage by day and move by night. Strictly day fighter-bomber units, F-80 and F-84 squadrons relied on information passed to them by the night intruder crews (flying USAF B-26s and Marine nightfighters) in order to locate truck convoys that had gone into hiding for the day.

By this point in the war the 8th FBG had all three of its F-80 squadrons in-theatre at Suwon, whilst the 51st FIG had discarded its Lockheed fighters (and the ground attack role) in favour of the new F-86E Sabre. The 49th FBG had also given up its Shooting Stars, although it remained very much a fighter-bomber unit thanks to its re-equipment with F-84s.

All of the units that had previously flown the F-80 had turned their aircraft over to the 8th FBG as they transitioned onto other aircraft types. And despite the group

suffering a relatively high attrition rate, it was usually able to sortie an impressive number of jets per mission.

Interdiction was the key to preventing the enemy from building up enough supplies to launch an offensive. Monitoring communist equipment levels was to prove difficult, however, for pilots rarely saw anything moving on the ground north of the frontline. One individual remembers that when he flew over terrain south of the frontline much activity could be seen, with the roads busy with traffic heading in both directions. However, once he crossed into enemy territory, there was no sign of human life at all – this held true all the way up to the Yalu River.

When strikes were carried out against known communist airfields, there were never any aircraft or repair crews to be seen. However, every fighter-bomber pilot knew that these areas came alive with men and machinery after dark, so they carried out their missions just as they had planned.

Having suffered heavy losses during the first Chinese offensive of the war, USAF Forward Air Controllers (FACs) now rarely ventured beyond the frontline with UN scouting patrols. However, from time to time they still managed to detect large concentrations of troops massing behind enemy lines, which indicated that there might be an attack launched against frontline positions.

BELOW *Kisarazu AB in Japan served both as the collecting centre for all obsolete aircraft that were being phased out of FEAF and the reception point for new replacement aircraft arriving from the USA. This photograph, taken in 1952, reveals a mix of three types on the flightline. Aside from the F-80C in the foreground, an F-51 can be seen parked to its left and two F-82 Twin Mustangs are parked in the background. The 'single-hole' Mustang had been replaced by the F-80, whilst the F-82's all-weather fighter role had passed to Lockheed's F-94 (Cale Herry)*

Here, Lt George Veazey of the 36th FBS recalls the sorties where his unit was called in to take care of suspected enemy troop build-ups;

'We used a similar set-up with our ordnance when we targeted enemy troops or repair crews that were repairing rail cuts. We would usually fly these missions on what was known as a "late light recce".

'We each carried two 500-lb and four 250-lb bombs. The latter were fragmentation bombs with worn out 0.5-in machine gun barrels screwed into the nose of each device, and with an instantaneous fuse in the bomb's tail. The idea was that when the ordnance hit the target, fragments would be scatter over a wide radius at high speed, mowing down any personnel that were close by.

'Typically, we would fly north just before sunset and drop the 500-lb bombs on a key junction or road, then fly north for about 15 minutes before returning to the point where we had initially dropped our ordnance. Road traffic would be jammed up waiting for the debris to be cleared, and at that point, we would dive down and drop the frags. This snarled things up even worse, greatly reducing

the distance that the convoys would be able to travel that night. Any damaged or disabled vehicles that were still around at dawn were easy pickings for the early flights.'

In several US government publications dating back to the mid-1950s, the final 18 months of the Korean War are referred to as having been a contest between the communist logistics corps and the UN fighter-bombers.

The Chinese had large numbers of troops available to throw into the fight against UN forces, but they could not hope to gain any ground without ample quantities of supplies and ammunition to support a major offensive. Typically, within ten miles of the MLR the communists would establish heavily-camouflaged supply dumps in an effort to build up logistical support to a level where it could sustain a major offensive. These sites were rarely detected from the air, but when they were, a unit (or group) strength effort was mounted to neutralise them.

Numerous success stories abounded following the lucky detection of such dumps during 1952-53. One such attack was recorded on 12 March 1952, which saw a group effort mounted by the 8th FBG – the post-mission

ABOVE *Bombed up and ready, but with no place to go! These 36th FBS F-80Cs have been grounded for the day due to the inclement weather. By late 1952, permanent sandbag revetments had been built at Suwon in order to provide an element of protection for aircraft parked on the flightline in the event of a nocturnal attack by Po-2s (Robert Crackel)*

photos revealed that the group had destroyed one of the largest supply dumps discovered during the entire Korean War. How this site came to be detected was not reported in the following press release;

'In a spectacular flexing of its combat muscle-power, the 8th FBG methodically smashed record after record. It flew a single day's high of 254 combat sorties, dropped 346,000 lbs of bombs, 43,000 gallons of napalm and fired 45,100 rounds of 0.50-calibre ammunition. The supply dumps were concentrated in a 50-square-mile area, which made it one of the largest of the war.'

The F-80 pilots had methodically worked their way from the perimeters of the dump to the centre, which was located around the village of Sinmak – the entire storage area was in a huge horseshoe-shaped valley. The first waves of aircraft, led by Lt Col Levi Chase (CO of the 8th FBG), followed a river that ran from Mulgae-ri to the target area south-east of Sinmak. From a distance, all the pilots could see was an innocent-looking collection of buildings that formed a typical Korean farming village. However, upon reaching the target area, pilots realised that the 'village' looked rather different to any other they had encountered in the past;

'The communists had piled supplies in small revetments terraced all along the hills. The stacks of supplies were bare on the sides, but they had been covered with fake straw roofs. We could plainly see the boxes neatly piled up. Most of the 8th's aircraft were loaded with napalm and 0.5-in ammunition. As our flights made their runs, we spread out and started burning everything from the outside in. We had enough napalm to cover most of the area', one of the attacking pilots later reported.

Flights from all three squadrons (35th, 36th and 80th FBSs) continued to work over the area for most of the day, with 2Lt David Ray, a 'Head Hunter' pilot with the 80th FBS, flying one of the last strikes;

'We were one of the last to hit the five- by ten-mile area, and as we approached the valley, it looked as though an atomic bomb had already hit the place. It was hard to tell if there was anything left untouched because there was a layer of heavy smoke and fire everywhere.'

Planning these missions was not easy. On paper, at least, it appeared that the group simply had to send every available F-80 to hit the target with as much ordnance as the jets could carry. However, to have put such a plan into practice would have resulted in major casualties for the attacking pilots, as the ridges that surrounded the target were heavily fortified with flak batteries.

These anti-aircraft guns had to be neutralised prior to the supply dump being attacked, so specific flak suppression flights (with aircraft carrying 500-lb GP bombs) were sent in minutes ahead of the main strike force. Leading one such flight was 1Lt Francis Walton of the 80th FBS;

OPPOSITE With the war in its final year, the 26th FIS on Okinawa continued to periodically rotate pilots and aircraft into the frontline in Korea. By then, the squadron's two sister-units had converted to the F-86E in Korea, so it supported the efforts of the 8th FBG (the only F-80 group left in-theatre) instead. Lt Wally Inscho is shown here by his aircraft at Naha AB, on Okinawa (Wally Inscho)

ABOVE *Most of the major maintenance work carried out on the 8th FBG's F-80s was done at Itazuke AB, although this routine engine change was taking place on the 36th FBS's flightline at Suwon (K-13) in the summer of 1952 (Don Brown)*

'It was our job to knock out the flak positions in order to clear the way for the guys carrying the napalm. We each carried four 500-lb bombs, and every time we'd hit the ridge line, the clouds of smoke would climb higher and higher into the sky! It looked like the entire ridge was blowing up. We got 100 per cent coverage. It was difficult to tell how many troop casualties we inflicted because the smoke and debris was so thick. Most of us flew three missions that day, and there is no doubt in my mind that this was the best series of sorties that I flew in.'

Twenty-four hours after this famous group effort, the 8th FBG's commander, Lt Col Chase, was asked to make a statement about the previous day's accomplishments;

'The most gratifying thing to me as commander of this outstanding fighter group was the spirit of everyone in the outfit, both officers and airmen. Wherever there was a bottleneck in the operations, everybody pitched in and solved it, thus keeping all of our aircraft in the air. They did a terrific job.

'I've experienced a lot of good shows, but this one was the best. We had no accidents and no losses to mar the day's splendid operations. It is a tribute to our maintenance crews that we had as many F-80s ready to fly at the end of the day as we did at the start!

'In the past, the 8th FBG had been restricted to a specific type of interdiction target. Fifth Air Force wanted to know just how effective we would be if our mission and target were suddenly changed. We were handed this target and told that the rest was up to us. We worked through the night planning where we would hit. You just don't go into a big area like that and start hunting. Every aircraft had a specific mission, and with the weather co-operating, we did a splendid job!'

As the war entered its final year, little changed in Korea. The Chinese knew they had no chance of pushing the UN forces off the peninsula, so their only hope was to capture a few miles of ground south of the 38th Parallel. Such a modest gain would allow North Korea to claim a psychological victory over its capitalist enemies.

Preparing for this offensive, the Chinese quickly amassed another enormous cache of supplies not far from the Sinmak dump that had been destroyed by the 8th FBG in March 1952. The new site was also detected by UN troops, and the FEAF ordered an immediate group-strength strike. Unlike the Sinmak attacks, the operation to destroy the new site would not end on such a positive note for the fighter-bomber force.

The missions took place on 26 May 1952, and one of the pilots sortied was the 80th FBS's 1Lt Richard Durkee;

'Our briefing for this mission was at 0330 hrs, and the entire complement of group pilots was present. We knew we would fly at least three missions that day, with our first one being flak suppression, followed by two with napalm. I was scheduled for the first two (flak suppression and napalm), and I would be serving as wingman for our new squadron commander on both strikes.

'Take off, rendezvous and navigation to the target area went without incident. We arrived at first light and immediately went into our bomb runs against the gun emplacements. Attacking in semi-darkness, we could see the red glow of the projectiles as they came up to meet us. We were probably having the same amount of lead thrown up at us during daylight attacks, but in this light we could actually see the rounds – and that was scary.

'Our suppression wasn't a big success, for there was more flak coming up at us when we left the area than when we had arrived! This indicated that either we didn't knock the guns out with our bombs, or that the Intelligence people did not know just how many of them were around the target. By the time we landed back at Suwon from the first strike, we all knew that the next two would be hot ones!

'We debriefed from the first mission and attended the briefing for mission number two. Once again, I would be flying on the wing of Maj Arthur Faunce, our new squadron CO. We arrived over the target area and started our descent to near-ground level so that we would be at the proper altitude for our napalm run. We were hoping that by coming in so low, we would enjoy the element of surprise.

'As we flew over the low hills and dropped down into the valley, we knew from the flak that our arrival had been no surprise – they were waiting for us! At our low scheduled airspeed it seemed we were standing still. The napalm drop was on target, and as my leader and I pulled up out of the valley, I spotted a small fire in the dive brake area on the underside of the CO's jet.

'I immediately called him on the radio and told him about it. He acknowledged the transmission, but seconds later I saw him punching off his external fuel tanks and, at the same time, he radioed in an excited voice that he was getting out!

'I pulled up alongside him to get a better look at the fire, by which time his aircraft was just starting to go from a nose-up attitude to a level position, although this soon changed to nose-down. We were flying in a left turn throughout this period. I observed that he had slumped forward in the cockpit, probably unconscious. With the jet's nose down at the low altitude we were flying, I knew that if he didn't regain consciousness quickly, it would be too late. As he approached the ground, I had to break away, but I kept yelling for him to pull up!

'Seconds later, he went into a hillside and his aircraft burst into a yellow-orange ball of flame. It was a tragic day

BELOW *Mission Centurions – 36th FBS pilots pose for a group shot after completing their 100th sortie of the war. They are all wearing their winter flying gear in an effort to stave off the extreme cold that Korea became famous for. This photograph was taken on 30 January 1952, in the midst of a major Chinese campaign to move supplies to the frontline under the cover of poor weather conditions (Clarence Hoggard)*

for our squadron, for we also lost 'B' Flight commander, 1Lt Robert Coffee. Seven other aircraft sustained heavy damage, although they all made it back to base. That day, after almost 50 years, is still etched in my memory just like it was yesterday!'

On 28 October 1952, the 8th FBG gained international attention when it logged its 50,000th combat sortie. The young pilot who had the honour of flying this milestone mission was 23-year-old 2Lt Warren R Guibor, who was flying one of 36 F-80s from the 8th FBG sent against troop concentrations in and around the Wonsan area. When Guibor landed, it triggered one of the biggest celebrations of the war.

Senior officers at Group HQ knew that this milestone was approaching, and they had already painted up the aircraft and hung banners prior to the strike group returning from the mission. This event secured media coverage in just about every newspaper in America, with the featured speaker at the festivities being Fifth Air Force commander, Lt Gen Glenn O Barcus.

The lion's share of the 50,000 sorties had been flown by the F-80s, although both the 35th and 36th FBSs had also used F-51 Mustangs during the early weeks of the war. By the time the war ended, the 8th had boosted its total to slightly over 63,000 combat sorties – a remarkable tribute to a great aircraft, and all of the troops that supported it! Incidentally, the two pilots that just missed completing the 50,000th sortie were 2Lt Gordon L

Edwards, who flew the 49,999th sortie, and 1Lt L R Hauser, who completed the 50,001st.

By now encountering very few visible targets during the day, the fighter-bombers became increasingly more reliant on Intelligence gathered from RF-80 photo missions, as well as feedback from the nocturnal B-26 units. For example, if there were any convoys damaged during the pre-dawn hours, this information was duly sent to FEAF HQ, who ordered a 'first light' mission to be launched to pick off any stragglers. The same worked for any trains that were caught short of the tunnels.

Despite the relative stalemate in the frontlines, the record sortie surges that were set by several squadrons were actually accomplished in the early months of 1953. The F-80 units deserved particular praise for their efforts, for they were flying some of the oldest aircraft in-theatre.

As the curtain slowly came down on the Shooting Star's action-packed career in Korea, it was the 80th FBS that momentarily diverted the media's attention away from the F-86 Sabre and focused it squarely on the unit's war-weary aircraft.

As far back as 11 March 1952, the 'Headhunters' had set a then unprecedented record of 96 sorties in a single day. This tally remained unbeaten until early April 1953, when Marine Air Group (MAG) 33 flew an amazing 117 sorties in one day – this mark would last slightly over two weeks. With the remaining F-80 fighter-bomber groups in Korea down to their last squadron, and the jet's combat

BELOW Maintenance crews have taken a break from changing yet another engine – this time the F-80C is from the 35th FBS. Flak damage was the main reason for so many engine changes at forward bases like Suwon, this being especially true for the F-80 and F-84 groups. The damaged engines were shipped back to maintenance facilities in Japan in order for repairs to be carried out, before being returned to Korea for further use (Richard Durkee)

career all but over, the 80th flew a record-shattering 120 sorties in a single day on 24 April 1953.

The setting of this record was not pre-planned or discussed in the pre-dawn briefings – it just seemed to take on a personality all of its own. By 0630 hrs, there were already 16 aircraft in the air returning from their early first-light strikes. This made for a solid foundation for a record attempt.

By the time the first wave had landed back at Suwon, FEAF's Combat Operations was calling in scores of targets from all over North Korea. At that time there was talk on the squadron about how well the day's sorties had gone so far, but MAG 33's tally was still a long way off. As wave after wave of F-80s departed Suwon, returning flights circled overhead, waiting for a chance to land. By the time these aircraft had taxied back into their revetments, the bomb trucks were already delivering ordnance to the flightline for the next wave. Everything seemed to be working perfectly.

It wasn't until the sun began to set that the unit's mission planners realised that they were only a few sorties short of breaking the record. It came down to the wire, and as the 80th FBS's CO later put it, 'If we had had just one abort, one plane out of commission for the day, then the entire effort would have been a failure – it was that close!'

Aircraft were turned around so quickly that one F-80 flew eight sorties that day and six others completed

seven. This was an outstanding performance when one bears in mind that some of these aircraft had been in combat for well over two years.

The squadron inflicted widespread damage during its 120 sorties, dropping 240 bombs for the day – 200 of them against targets spread along the entire length of the frontline, and the remaining 40 well into North Korea. The official FEAF press release stating the damage done by the 80th FBS on this day read as follows;

'1115 yards of trenches damaged, 13 caves damaged, six caves destroyed, 33 bunkers damaged, 19 mortar positions damaged, ten personnel shelters destroyed, numerous gun positions damaged, seven secondary explosions after hits on ammo dumps, along with numerous other targets damaged or destroyed.'

Weather conditions on this day were perfect for ground attack sorties, with pilots encountering negligible wind, which further increased the accuracy of their bombing runs. Admittedly, smoke and dust created by previous explosions lingered over the target areas, delaying incoming flights from dropping their bombs by a few minutes. The accurate target descriptions given by the T-6 Mosquito pilots allowed the fighter-bombers to identify and hit their targets quickly, facilitating a rapid return to base for re-loading.

This combination of aggressive F-80 pilots, experienced Mosquito pilots and the Army's target marking artillery led to over 100 close support missions being

LEFT *This 25th FIS jet was riddled with automatic weapons fire as it pulled out of a dive-bombing run through a valley in North Korea – the gun positions were sited on nearby ridges. If the gunner had led his target a little more, the damage would have been centred around the cockpit, and that could have been disastrous (H P Saabye)*

MAIN PICTURE *Loaded with 1000-lb GP bombs, this 80th FBS Shooting Star taxies out from its parking area toward the main runway. At the controls is Lt Don Culver. Behind the jet is an ex-35th FBS F-80C now being flown by the 'Headhunters'. The 35th had already begun transitioning over to the F-86F by the time this photograph was taken in early 1953*
(James Buchanan)

INSET *This group of elite pilots flew the final F-80 missions of the war, their yellow caps indicating that they all belonged to the 80th FBS. This Shooting Star is yet another ex-35th FBS jet (Robert Odle)*

RIGHT *All the various units within the F-80 groups had their own signs posted in front of their respective buildings. This particular 'Headhunter' sign hung in front of the Armament Section's Headquarters at Suwon – the shack was located next to the 80th FBS's flightline. This caricature served as the official squadron emblem (Bill Nowadnick)*

successfully flown on this day. And none of the attacking Shooting Stars received even the slightest damage. Of the remaining 20 aircraft that flew sorties north of the MLR on this day, two F-80s reported battle damage but none were lost. Ironically, those machines that were hit were participating in the first and last flights of the day!

On the 'first light' mission, 2Lt Richard Housum was strafing a line of trucks when his jet was struck in the nose by automatic weapons fire. And during the 'last light recce', the F-80 of 2Lt Donald W Culver was damaged while dive-bombing a bridge. A single 40 mm round punctured its fuselage, although this failed to prevent Culver from safely returning to Suwon.

As an example of how motivated the entire unit was on this day, maintenance crews repaired Lt Housum's jet in time for it to participate in a sortie (with another pilot at the controls) flown just eight hours after it was hit!

The real unsung heroes of 24 April 1953 were the crew chiefs, the armourers and various other support personnel. Indeed, without them, the record would never have been broken! Flying 20 airworthy F-80s, the 80th FBS's 120-sortie surge was completed without a single abort, which in itself is the biggest compliment that a dedicated groundcrew could receive.

On innumerable occasions, less than ten minutes after an aircraft had recovered from a mission, another pilot would be climbing up the ladder to strap into the still warm cockpit to fly yet another mission. Some pilots commented that if they stopped to chat with someone for a few minutes, before reporting to debriefing, they would see the aircraft they had just landed, taxi out with

a full bomb load! This meant that the jet had been fuelled and armed with 2000 lbs of bombs in around 20 minutes.

The 24th was truly a pilots' day, for only two of the 29 that sortied flew less than three missions – under normal conditions, a pilot might get to fly two missions in a day. Even the 80th FBS's Operations Officer, Maj George R Halliwell, got in a 'last light' armed recce mission. He had spent the entire day scheduling aircraft and pilots, and was only able to break away for the sortie when the record was 'in the bag'.

The final mission tally recorded that four pilots flew three sorties, eleven flew four, ten flew five and two took top honours with six sorties apiece. The two with top time – 1Lts Arthur D Violette Jr and Theodore A Platz Jr – tied an existing record that had been set by a T-6 Mosquito pilot from the 6167th Tactical Reconnaissance Group.

24 April 1953 was a classic example of the F-80 Shooting Star, and its support personnel, performing at their very best. Today, 50 years on from the Korean War, survivors of the conflict still fondly recall their time flying or maintaining Lockheed's Shooting Star. Perhaps 8th FBG veteran John W Keeler (who flew F-80C 49-779) sums it up best in the following quote;

'Perhaps someday, in some aviation museum, we will be able to see examples of all the great fighters, and as we pause before the Shooting Star on exhibit, I'll say to the boy standing by my side, "Son, your dad flew that one when it was the best fighter-bomber aircraft in the world!" And who knows, maybe we'll be looking at my 'ole Seven-Seven-Nine!'

BELOW *Throughout the Korean War, the 8th FBG's commanding officers flew combat missions in their own assigned aircraft, which featured a special paint scheme displaying the colours of all three operational squadrons within the group. Here, Lt Col Levi Chase's F-80C has been loaded with napalm and four 5-in rockets. Note that the 'CO's stripes' have also been added to the jet's tip tanks (Richard Durkee)*

These two 80th FBS aircraft are seen in the process of being 'turned around' for another mission. The crew chief is taking care of the paperwork near the nosewheel of FT-797, while the bomb truck slowly makes its way down the flightline to reload aircraft that are scheduled to participate in the next mission. FT-797 was assigned to Lt Richard T Durkee (Richard Durkee)

RIGHT *The 36th FBS painted some elaborate nose-art on a number of its aircraft towards the end of the war, with* "EVIL EYE FLEAGLE" *being one of the most colourful. Its nickname was derived from a popular American cartoon character of the time. These two F-80s had just returned from a mission, and were waiting for the maintenance crews to arrive to refuel and rearm them. Note that the crew chief of FT-547 has already made a start on turning his jet around (Gene Zehr)*

ABOVE The last group of pilots to see combat in the F-80 pose on the flightline at Suwon. The 80th FBS traded its final Shooting Stars in for new F-86F Sabres shortly after this photograph was taken. All three squadrons controlled by the 8th FBG had pilots who were close to finishing their tours when the transition to the Sabre was made, and these men were allowed to shift to the 80th FBS to complete their final sorties in the F-80. Those who still had a significant number of missions to fly moved on to the new F-86 (James Buchanan)

LEFT Lt Warren R Guibor of the 80th FBS taxies in to a special area on the Suwon flightline that had been set up to mark the celebration of the 8th FBG's 50,000th combat sortie of the Korean War. This landmark flight occurred on 28 October 1952, when the group attacked troops close to Wonsan. Some 36 F-80s from the 8th FBG participated in the mission (Robert Veazey)

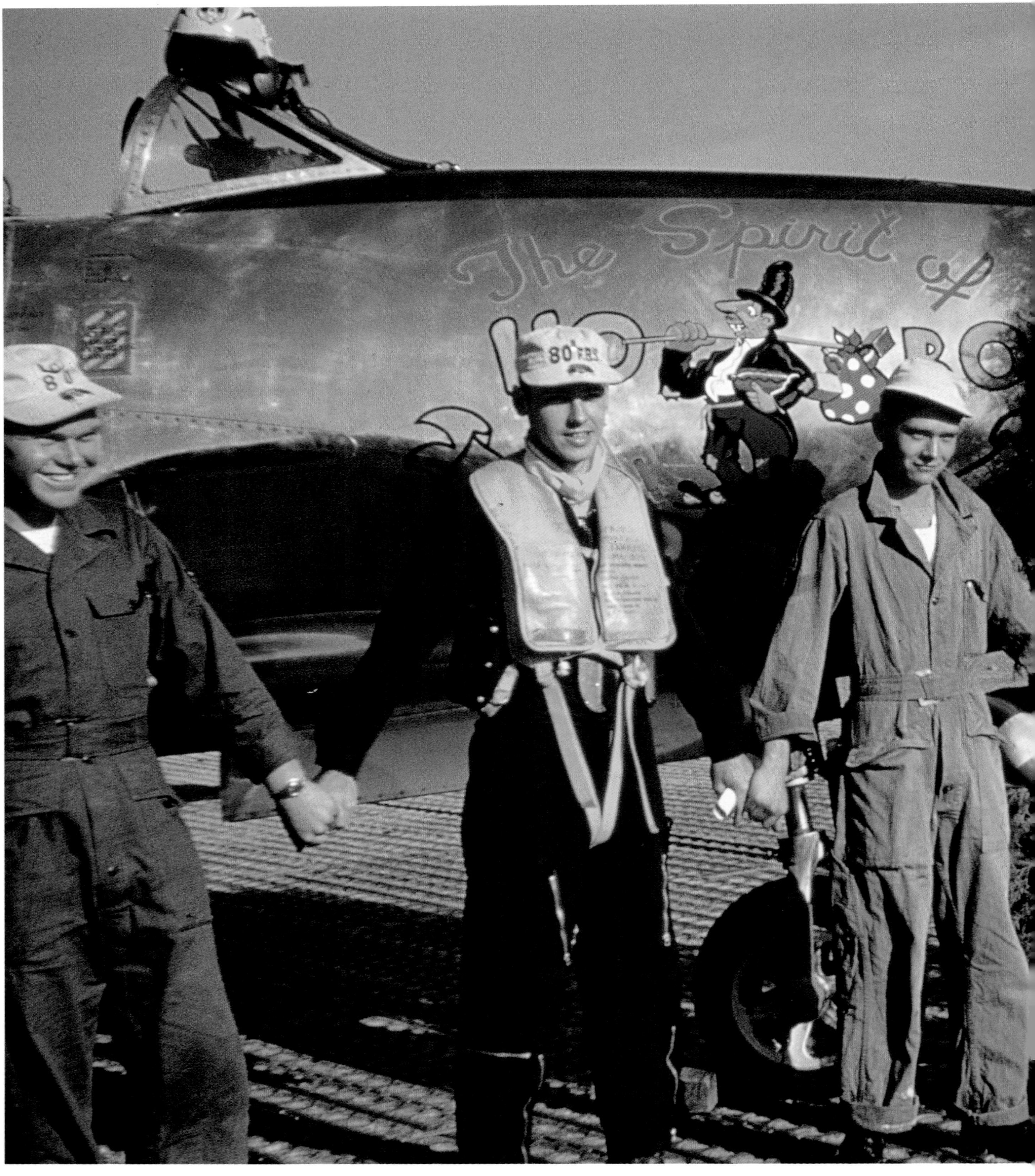
The Spirit of

Every pilot that ever flew a combat mission in any war knew that it was the maintenance crews that kept the aircraft in the air. For the most part, these individuals have been omitted from the media attention lavished upon aviators in conflict. This was not the case when the 8th FBG honoured its 50,000th sortie, however, for the pilot, Lt Warren Guibor, posed for a series of press photographs with his entire groundcrew (Warren Guibor)

INSET LEFT *Celebrations marking the the 8th FBG's acclaimed 50,000th combat sortie continued long after the aircraft had landed. Here, senior officers from the FEAF address VIPs and air- and groundcrews from the group. By the time the war ended in July 1953, the 8th had completed no fewer than 63,000 sorties in Korea (Richard Durkee)*

INSET RIGHT *The heavy snows during the winter of 1952-53 had little effect on F-80 operations, for units continued to put pressure on the Chinese truck convoys that were trying to take advantage of the inclement weather. These 36th FBS machines have been loaded with 1000-lb bombs in preparation for their next mission (Robert Crackel)*

MAIN PICTURE *An unidentified 36th FBS pilot climbs out of the cockpit of "EVIL EYE FLEAGLE" after completing a mission over snow-covered North Korea. By early 1953 there were just 70 F-80Cs still in Korea, and they were all flown by the 8th FBG (Tom Owen)*

35th FBS 'Black Panther' pilot Lt Frank Ray prepares to climb the ladder into the cockpit of his F-80C at the start of another mission. The 35th and 36th FBSs turned their Shooting Stars over to the 80th FBS once they commenced their transition onto the F-86F in early 1953 (Frank Ray)

RIGHT *Lt Jack Taylor poses alongside a fearsome looking 36th FBS machine in the snow at Suwon in early 1953. The unit briefly boasted several similarly-painted Shooting Stars in 1952-53, although the shark's teeth were quickly removed following orders to this effect from 8th FBG HQ. Lt Taylor is wearing a 'Poopy Suit', which protected the pilot from the frigid cold should he be forced down over water (Jack Taylor)*

ABOVE 6 GUNS FOR HIRE *was the personal mount of 80th FBS pilot Lt Gene Zehr, seen here climbing out of the cockpit of the jet. His crew chief is giving him the 'welcome back' sign after the completion of a long mission (Gene Zehr)*

LEFT *The 8th FBG commander's colourful F-80C has been loaded with an unusual array of ordnance – two 500-lb and four 250-lb bombs. Note the 8th FBG emblem painted on the nose of the aircraft (Richard Durkee)*

FAF 9PF-115
AIR FORCE MODEL F780C-10-LO
AIR FORCE SERIAL NO. 49-817

Lt George R Veazey and his Joanie's MODELEER have their picture taken together just moments before he climbed aboard at the start of a mission from Suwon. Veazey's Pilot Training Class 52-B saw 98 pilots graduate, of which 19 lost their lives in action over Korea and three were made PoWs (George R Veazey)

RIGHT *This flight of four F-80s was comprised of jets from the 35th (blue) and 36th (red) FBSs. Such a mix was commonplace in the final 18 months of the war, as the 8th FBG's trio of units operated as one oversized squadron. Some of the missions flown from Suwon to the frontlines lasted less than one hour, depending on how many different targets the T-6 Mosquito pilots wanted them to hit (Fred Kummer)*

BELOW RIGHT *When warm weather arrived in Korea, the maintenance crews stripped down to either T-shirts or bare skin in an effort to counter the high temperatures that became synonymous with the summers in this region. These 36th FBS groundcrews are finishing up the reload cycle for the 0.5-in guns (George R Veazey)*

OPPOSITE *Kiss of Fire was one of the more colourful F-80s in the 36th FBS. In early 1953 at least seven aircraft received special attention from one of the unit's artists. The 36th FBS pilot shown here is Lt Frank Ray, who flew the aircraft on several missions (Frank Ray)*

CHAPTER FIVE
TACTICAL RECONNAISSANCE ROLE

FEAF press releases proudly boasted in 1949 and early 1950 that there were 365 F-80 Shooting Stars in the Far East. However, they failed to mention that there were only 25 RF-80As in-theatre, and that this meagre force would find itself hard-pressed to satisfy the demand for aerial photographs generated by the communist invasion of South Korea.

All RF-80As in the Far East were flown by the 8th Tactical Reconnaissance Squadron (TRS), which was based at Yokota under the command of the 35th FBG. Once fighting started in Korea, the FEAF found that the RF-80 was the best platform for securing quality imagery of the NKPA's invading force. This effectively meant that the unit had to deal with virtually all of the UN's reconnaissance requirements during the first few weeks of war.

UN forces had no clear picture of what the situation in Korea was like for the first 48 hours of the invasion, and the Fifth Air Force's efforts to rectify this were hampered by the poor weather that blanketed the peninsula.

On the evening of 27 June the 8th TRS moved four of its RF-80s from Yokota down to Itazuke, the latter being the closest major air base to South Korea. By the time the jets had completed their base move, the weather front had shifted to the south, and it was clearing up over the Seoul/Kimpo area.

Desperate for accurate intelligence, FEAF ordered the 8th to launch an RF-80 to take photos of the roads around Seoul. Lt Bryce Poe II was selected to crew the jet, and he, officially, became the first American pilot to fly a combat reconnaissance mission in the Korean War.

By the time Lt Poe reached his target area, the weather had cleared to such an extent that he was able to take some excellent photographs. Now, for the first time, the war planners in Tokyo were able to see just how

RIGHT *Lt Norm Fredkin (left) and Lt Keith Brown take a break between sorties on the flightline at Kimpo in the spring of 1952. RF-80s usually had an F-86 escort when they ventured into the extreme northern sectors of Korea due to MiG-15 activity in this area. The MiG pilots proved to be unusually aggressive when it came to attacking the RF-80s, because they knew they could not shoot back. The aircraft with the yellow band on the vertical stabiliser is from the 15th TRS, whilst the jet with the red sunburst on the tail is a conventional F-80C assigned to the 36th FBS (Norm Fredkin)*

critical the situation was following the development of Poe's film. Within hours of seeing evidence of the extent of the invasion, UN strike planners had prioritised key targets and launched numerous flights of fighter-bombers to hit troop concentrations in the area that had been photographed. Poe recalls that memorable day;

'I was called in while the strikes were being carried out. They didn't waste any time in gleaning information from the film I had taken that morning. I was told to fly a follow-up sortie to film the damage that these early strikes had generated. I made a fast run over an enemy bristling with anti-aircraft fire, and I can't really recall much of what happened. I do remember, however, that there were countless burning trucks and smoke billowing skyward. The fighter-bombers had done a great job.'

For the first ten weeks of the war, most of the Korean Peninsula was considered to be enemy territory, which put undue pressure on the 8th TRS because of the vast area of terrain it now had to monitor. The North Koreans were using at least four major road routes to re-supply their troops in the southern tip of the country, and although hard pressed to cover each of these, at least the RF-80 pilots knew that enemy aircraft would not be one of the hazards they faced when flying these missions.

Indeed, the greatest problems facing the 8th TRS were all maintenance-related, for its overworked groundcrews were struggling to keep the unit's handful of RF-80s airworthy.

In order to gain the upper hand in a war such as this one, planners had to have accurate up-to-date photos of enemy strengths and movements. Only the RF-80 could provide these images, and the 25 jets in-theatre were immediately given top priority for spare parts. And when the unit lost an aircraft through attrition or to heavy maintenance, a replacement RF-80 was immediately brought in from the US.

During August 1950, the amount of troops and equipment being hauled down from Pyongyang was minimal. This was due to the fact that everything the North Koreans had was thrown against the Pusan Perimeter. However, there was a steady stream of food and ammunition making its way down all of the supply routes.

One of the first facts revealed by the film shot by the 8th TRS was that the communist supply lines had to be severed in order to ease the pressure on UN troops in the frontline forces. This became the top priority of F-51s and F-80s, with the Mustangs in particular being very effective in this role due to their proximity to the action from bases at Pohang and Pusan – less than five minutes' flying time from the frontline.

Relief for the beleaguered troops on the Korean Peninsula was in sight, however, thanks to the planners of

BELOW Two high-flying RF-80s from the 15th TRS join up after completing their photo-runs over North Korea. This shot was taken during the first year of the war, when the squadron was operating out of Taegu AB (Bill Nimmo)

ABOVE *The 8th TRS was responsible for undertaking all long-range RF-80 missions during the early stages of the Korean War. Lacking a suitable base in-theatre, the unit was forced to fly out of Itazuke AB, heading all the way up to the Yalu and back on many of these missions. This 8th TRS 'photo-bird' is pictured on the ramp at Itazuke in a typical configuration for the period – elongated 'Misawa' tanks fitted to the wing tips and further external tanks on the inner wing pylons. The RF-80 could not perform its mission without all of this additional fuel, for sufficient reserves were needed to allow the pilot to depart North Korea at high speed (Carl Ebneter)*

the Inchon Landing. For the US Marine Corps' First Division to succeed with this audacious invasion, it needed up to date photos of Inchon Harbour – the only ones in existence had been taken in 1948 by an RF-61C Black Widow, again flown by the 8th TRS. These did not reveal the highs and lows of the tides, so RF-80s teamed up with Marine F4U-5Ps and F7F-3Ps to take detailed pictures from every angle at certain times of the day.

The 8th TRS flew four precisely-timed photo missions in two days, the RF-80 pilots having to secure imagery with their oblique cameras at a dangerously low altitude. Once in possession of the tidal information they required, the planners came up with an effective landing strategy and the Marines did the rest. Within 24 hours of finishing the photo runs, over 2000 copies of these photographs had been delivered to the assembling Task Force at Kobe Naval Base in Japan. The landing proved to be very successful, and the spearhead to the east broke the North Korean supply lines, triggering a rapid communist retreat toward the 38th Parallel.

For the first six months of the war, the 8th TRS operated under greater pressure than any other unit in the FEAF – its pilots also flew greater distances to complete their missions, being based in Japan. The few airfields in South Korea boasting suitable facilities for jet operations were made available exclusively to F-80 fighter-bomber groups for much of 1950.

To make matters worse for the already hard-pressed recce pilots, on 1 November the first examples of the MiG-15 were encountered near the Chinese border. Early that morning a lone B-26, and its T-6 forward air controller, had been jumped by a swarm of Yak fighters in the Yangsi area. A flight of F-51s patrolling nearby answered their call for help and shot down two of the enemy fighters.

An RF-80 was immediately despatched to take pictures of the closest enemy air base to where this action had taken place, and the photographs revealed 15 enemy fighters parked on the field. Twelve F-80Cs were launched to destroy the aircraft and render the airfield inoperable. It proved to be a very difficult target to neutralise, for the revetments in which the aircraft were parked faced Manchuria, so to properly set up for the bomb run, the F-80s were exposed to intense anti-aircraft fire from both sides of the river.

And it was during the course of the airfield attack that a flight of F-51s was jumped by six MiG-15s just a few miles away.

From that date on, it became very dangerous for an unarmed aircraft to venture into the area, which was quickly dubbed 'MiG Alley'. For the RF-80, speed was its greatest defence, but the MiG-15 was at least 200 mph faster – such a speed difference would extract gallons of sweat from numerous RF-80 pilots!

One such individual was Lt Francis W Meyer, who recalls a memorable encounter that he and his wingman had with a pair of MiG-15s north of Pyongyang;

'Our mission for the day was to photograph the main rail line from Pyongyang northward to Sinanju right after it had been hit by fighter-bombers. Due to the danger from the MiGs, when we worked up in this area we always sent two aircraft – one to take the pictures and the other to keep an eye out for enemy fighters. This was my 20th combat mission, and my first encounter with any of the MiGs.

'Having completed my photo run with my wingman, Lt Dick McNulty, up on the perch, we reversed so he could take his pictures. Approaching Sinanju, I was indicating about 50 mph above McNulty's speed. As observer pilot, you would be all over the sky watching for

MiGs, and this manoeuvring would get you behind the lead unless you increased your speed.

'I was in a left turn checking our tail, and had just started to reverse my turn to the right, when I noticed a white trail like a contrail. We were at 21,000 ft, which was much too low for contrails. About this time, I hear Dick shout over the radio "BREAK RIGHT FRANK". My adrenaline cut in and I panicked, breaking left then right in a dive for lower altitude.

'Just before I did break right, an orange fireball about the size of a grapefruit passed within a few feet of my canopy, followed by a MiG-15 overshooting me in a climb in an effort to make another pass at me! The pilot was looking down at me, and he was wearing a leather helmet and goggles.

'Whilst in my dive I jettisoned the tip tanks so I could be more manoeuvrable. I called out to Dick to check on my MiG's position, and he replied he was shaking a MiG off his tail, and that the one that was after me had flown into one of my tip tanks right after I let them go – this was never confirmed of course. This episode was over in

seconds, but I will never forget it! We did accomplish our mission with some good pictures.'

On 25 February 1951, the tactical reconnaissance operation in Korea became better organised with the activation of the 67th Tactical Reconnaissance Wing (TRW). This marked the demise of the 8th TRS, as it would now be known as the 15th TRS, equipped with the RF-80. Also included within this new wing was the 45th TRS (RF-51/F-51) and the 12th TRS (RB-26), the latter unit having the responsibility of operating at night.

From October 1950 until late February 1951, the reconnaissance mission had been controlled by the 543rd Tactical Support Group, based at Taegu. The 67th TRW duly established its first base here too, once the Chinese advances had been checked and the frontline stabilised.

Although the Taegu facility was one of the crudest in Korea at the time, it served the wing well until crowded conditions at Kimpo (K-14) were eased by the opening of other airfields. Finally, on 22 August 1951, the 67th established its main HQ at the latter base, and it would remain here until the war's end.

LEFT A group of recce pilots from the 15th TRS 'Cotton Pickers' pose for the camera on the flightline at Kimpo AB in the spring of 1952 (Norm Fredkin)

The 45th TRS adopted its distinctive 'Polka Dots' after it had moved to Kimpo AB with its veteran RF-51s, the marking also later featuring on its RF-80s. The unit commenced transitioning onto the RF-80 in June 1952, although a number of Mustangs remained on strength until year-end. This 45th TRS machine was photographed during a visit to Taegu AB in late 1952. Note the unit emblem painted on its fuselage (Otto Kopf)

Legendary leader of the 67th TRW, Col Karl L 'Pop' Polifka, was the most respected expert on tactical reconnaissance within the USAF, and one of its most competent leaders. Unfortunately, his tenure did not last long, for he was killed while flying a dangerous low-level mission in an RF-51 on 1 July 1951. The wing had two interim commanders before Col Edwin Chickering was brought in on 31 October 1951.

One of the first changes made by Chickering was to begin phasing out the Mustangs in favour of more RF-80s (issued to the 45th TRS). Like Polifka, he believed in flying the same missions as his men, and making as many passes over the target as it took to get the required pictures.

By early 1951 RF-80s could usually rely on an F-86 escort when flying over enemy territory. However, even with the Sabres in attendance, recce pilots never considered any mission over North Korea to be a 'milk-run'. For example, if there were enough MiGs 'out and about' to outnumber the escort, there was always the chance that one would break through the barrier and go after the defenceless RF-80. This happened to 15th TRS pilot 2Lt Norman Fredkin;

'My mission was to take close-up pictures of enemy airfields at Sinuiju and Uiju, located right up on the river, not far from the big MiG base at Antung. We had to find out if these bases had been repaired to the point where they were serviceable.

'After a problem-free briefing, pre-flight and take-off, I began thinking about the dangerous mission ahead, and if I was going make the rendezvous with my F-86 escort on time. As I flew deeper and deeper into North Korea, the

radio silence was broken when I heard, "Have you in sight Dog One – proceed on course". My escorts had picked me up and were in place somewhere above me.

'Whilst concentrating on navigating my way to the enemy airfields by the shortest possible route, I heard a few disconcerting transmissions in my headset. "Fifteen Bogeys three o'clock level. Contrails six o'clock high. Orange flight break right!" My escorts obviously had their hands full!

'Suddenly, my target came in sight and I turned into it level at 20,000 ft. The skies ahead became dotted with pretty black and orange puffs. Once over the target, with the cameras running, I ignored everything around me except the target run. Then I heard another transmission from Sabre lead. "Dog One, two bogeys at your eight o'clock and closing". I was just about finished with my photo run, so I ignored the warning. Seconds later, "Break left Dog One NOW! Can't cover you – turn tighter, tighter! Flip your tip tanks damn it!". Before the sentence was finished, my hand was already pulling the tip release as I continued breaking hard into a pair of MiG-15s.

'Suddenly, my aircraft lurched violently as only one tip tank came off, causing the jet to snap uncontrollably over and over. Everything went black! Somewhere in this violence, the other tip tank fell off and the aircraft began to right itself. My vision was now making the transition from black to grey, and then after a few seconds my vision was back. Analysing the situation, I had lost several thousand feet and I was diving earthward, with my airspeed well beyond the red line!

'The aircraft was buffeting like a leaf in a gale and the stick was jumping around the cockpit like you wouldn't believe. In short order, I regained control of the aircraft and dived down to the deck, before heading south with an IAS of over 500 mph. Looking around, the MiGs were nowhere in sight, and I don't believe any aircraft could have kept up with me during all those gyrations! In minutes I was back in the pattern to land at Kimpo, and all of a sudden, the events of the past few minutes seemed to be in the distant past. Now, all I had to do was get the film in to the lab, where hopefully the shots required would be developed!'

BELOW By the late autumn of 1951, Korean labourers had begun constructing sandbag revetments at Kimpo to protect aircraft of the 67th TRW and 4th FIW (F-86s). Operating in less than salubrious conditions, this 'high-timer' RF-80 is having its cameras loaded in preparation for another photo mission over North Korea. The black RB-26s in the background belonged to the 12th TRS (James Hanson)

In reading some of the dogfight accounts from the F-86 Sabre pilots in Korea, it quickly becomes obvious that their communist opponents in the MiG-15 greatly varied in ability. The ones that seemed to be exceptionally good were referred to as 'Honchos', whilst the rest flew like students at varying levels in their training. Some of the more aggressive students were turned loose on the conventional propeller-driven types and the recce aircraft. And although the RF-80 was a capable opponent, MiG pilots knew full well that it had no guns. On at least one mission north of Pyongyang, the enemy pilots' inexperience was glaringly evident, and it led to their death.

In the autumn of 1952 two RF-80s were tasked with flying a mission close to the Yalu. They went about their business as usual, with one flying look-out while the second jet took pictures. Capts Anthony Katauski and George Aiken were suddenly jumped by a pair of MiG-15s. Katauski recalls the mission;

'Two enemy fighters came up behind us as we were carrying out our photo-runs. We both went into a steep dive and they followed. They were probably concentrating on keeping us in their sights. Capt Aiken and I took them straight down to tree-top level, and as we got right above the tree line, we pulled up sharply.

'Evidently, they didn't realise how close we were to the ground, because they abruptly disappeared and we didn't see them anymore. We returned to base safely and without any other problems. The next day, an aerial reconnaissance of the area turned up the burned out wreckage of two MiGs that had gone down close to each other. I guess their inexperience caught up with them, and we were lucky.'

Of the thousands of missions flown by the 8th and 15th TRSs during the course of the war, most followed a set pattern. Indeed, there were very few, if any, that stood out in the minds of most pilots. Each and every photo run had to be made at a set altitude and speed, allowing flak gunners to get an accurate fix on them.

By far the most memorable missions were those where pilots had to contend with MiG-15s, and their deadly 37 mm cannon armament. One lucky hit could bring instant death, or force a bail out in bitterly cold temperatures hundreds of miles into enemy territory – many recce pilots simply vanished as a result of the enemy's defences, never to be heard from again. Most had probably experienced the full impact of the MiG's cannon, or been on the receiving end of a well-aimed large-calibre burst of flak.

BELOW *15th TRS pilot Lt Gene Newnam stands on the wing of his assigned RF-80, which was nicknamed SHUTTER BUG. This photograph was taken just prior to Newnam heading north on a mission from Kimpo in early 1953. The RF-80 was 200 mph slower than the MiG-15, so it was extremely vulnerable to attack when flying north of Pyongyang (Gene Newnam)*

LEFT *The working conditions at all bases in South Korea were generally poor for the duration of the war, and harsh winter weather did not help matters. Indeed, the moving parts within the RF-80's battery of cameras were particularly affected by cold and wet weather. Forced to work in the open in near blizzard conditions, these crewmen are seen trying to get film loaded and ready for a mission over the main supply routes in late 1952. The Chinese were using the inclement weather to mask the movement of larger quantities of supplies to the frontline. Once the pictures revealed what the communists were up to, the fighter-bombers were unleashed on the enemy truck columns (Gene Newnam)*

BELOW LEFT *Lt Joe Lanahan performs his pre-flight inspection on the Kimpo ramp prior to flying a photo-mission over North Korea. Note the large number of mission symbols that adorn the fuselage of* Betty Fay *just forward of the cockpit. The all-black RB-26s parked behind the RF-80 were flown by the 12th TRS (Joe Lanahan)*

This RF-80 is in the process of having its engine started at Kimpo early one morning during the winter of 1951-52. The crew chief (standing on the starboard wing root) and other support personnel can be seen keeping a watchful eye on proceedings. The Mustangs in the background belonged to the 45th TRS (James Hanson)

ABOVE One of the most colourful RF-80s flown by the 15th TRS was BALL-O-FIRE, shown here taxying out to the main runway at Kimpo in the early spring of 1953. The MiG threat was at its greatest at this point in the war, with large numbers of communist jet fighters being encountered over the Yalu. Fortunately for the recce pilots, F-86s were usually available in sufficient numbers to offer protection (Gene Newnam)

RIGHT All RF-80s in the FEAF pre-war were owned by the 8th TRS at Misawa, Japan. They boasted few markings, and this early model (seen in 1948) was probably one of the aircraft that later flew some of the first missions over Korea in July 1950 (Tom Gerzel)

LEFT *Lt Ted Gesling, shown here at Kimpo at war's end, was a typical 15th TRS pilot in that he had flown numerous sorties in both the RF-80 and the RF-86. His unit left Korean soil in early March 1954 and set up operations at Komaki AB, in Japan (Ted Gesling)*

MAIN PICTURE *By the final weeks of the conflict, both of the reconnaissance types shown here at Kimpo were regularly flying daylight photo-missions deep into North Korea. The RF-86 rarely needed a fighter escort, for it was fast enough to avoid any intercepting MiG-15s. Both types were operated side-by-side within the 15th TRS (Ted Gesling)*

INSET *The appearance of the brand new RF-80A in the Far East created much interest amongst attendees at the type's first Air Force Day Open House at Itazuke AB in September 1948. The 8th TRS had replaced its World War 2-vintage Northrop RF-61Cs with 25 RF-80As literally weeks prior to the open house. These self-same jets would provide the backbone of the FEAF's tactical reconnaissance force when NKPA invaded South Korea on 25 June 1950 (Charles D Chitty)*

Appendices

CONFIRMED F-80 AIR-TO-AIR KILLS IN KOREA

Date	Aircraft Type	Unit	Pilot
27 June 1950	Il-10 (x2)	35th FBS	Lt Robert E Wayne
27 June 1950	Il-10	35th FBS	Capt Ray Schillereff
27 June 1950	Il-10	35th FBS	Lt Robert Dewald
29 June 1950	Il-10	8th FBG	Lt Roy Marsh
30 June 1950	Yak-9	36th FBS	Lt J B Thomas
30 June 1950	Yak-9	36th FBS	Lt Charles Wurster
7 July 1950	Yak-9	39th FIS	Lt Robert A Coffin
17 July 1950	Yak-9	35th FBS	Lt Francis B Clark
19 July 1950	Yak-9	36th FBS	Lt Robert D McKee
19 July 1950	Yak-9	36th FBS	Lt Elwood A Kees
19 July 1950	Yak-9	36th FBS	Lt Charles Wurster
20 July 1950	Yak-9	35th FBS	Lt Robert L Lee
20 July 1950	Yak-9	35th FBS	Lt David H Goodnough
8 November 1950	MiG-15	16th FIS	Lt Russell J Brown
17 March 1951	MiG-15	36th FBS	Lt Howard J Landry
29 July 1951	MiG-15	16th FIS	Lt William W McAllister

Total Confirmed Air-to-Air Kills – 17

LOCKHEED F-80C SHOOTING STAR

Powerplant
one Allison J33-A-35 single shaft centrifugal turbojet, rated at 5400-lb (2450-kg) thrust

Performance
maximum speed, 590-606 mph (950-975 km/h)
initial climb approx. 5000 ft (1524 m) per minute
service ceiling approx. 48,000 ft (14,630 m)
range 1100-1250 miles (1770-2000 km)

Weights
empty, 8240 lb (3741 kg)
maximum loaded, 15,336 lb (6963 kg)

Dimensions
Span: 38 ft 10.5 in (11.85 m)
Length: 34 ft 6 in (10.51 m)
Height: 11 ft 8 in (3.55 m)

Armament
six 0.5-in Colt-Browning M-3 machine guns fitted in the nose; various underwing stores including 250-, 500- and 1000-lb HE GP bombs, napalm and 5-in High-Velocity Aerial Rockets (HVARs)

UNIT CITATION

Every F-80 group that saw combat in the Korean War received a Distinguished Unit Citation. These were not given out at random, but were earned the hard way. The following is a verbatim copy of FEAF/HQ's General Order Number 93, issued on 8 March 1951 in the name of the President of the United States, for the outstanding contribution and record that was compiled by the 49th FBG:

The 49th FBG is cited for extraordinary heroism and fidelity during the period 27 June to 25 November 1950. The 49th Group especially distinguished itself as the first jet fighter organisation to operate actively in the combat field. This operation, unparalleled in the history of the US Air Force, extended the effective striking range of the F-80 aircraft in excess of 200 miles over previous operations from air bases in Japan. The resulting increases in combat sorties, savings in fuel and ability to remain over enemy territory for greater periods were inestimable contributions to the United Nations effort.

The outstanding service rendered by this organisation while flying over 9664 combat sorties in close support of the United Nations forces is strikingly demonstrated by the following record of damage and destruction inflicted on the enemy: 27 aircraft, 239 tanks, 105 vehicles, 94 locomotives, 1706 rail cars and 2900 miscellaneous targets including bridges, supply dumps and vessels.

Despite the necessity of relocating assigned units on four separate occasions, the 49th FBG has provided continuous combat effort with undiminished effectiveness. Valuable information relative to capabilities, limitations and behaviour of jet fighter aircraft under actual combat conditions was compiled by this organisation, materially increasing subsequent operational effectiveness in the Korean conflict and providing standard operational procedures for future operations.

The aerial achievements of this organisation are resplendent with repeated acts of heroism, gallantry and high personal courage. The impressive total of 17,625 combat hours flown by this organisation is indicative of the high calibre and skill of maintenance and ground personnel. Operating under adverse and hazardous conditions on a continuous daily schedule, the officers and airmen of the 49th FBG performed in such a manner as to reflect the greatest credit on the organisation, the Far East Air Forces and the United States Air Force.

By Command of Lieutenant General
George E Stratemeyer

Lockheed F-80B Shooting Star

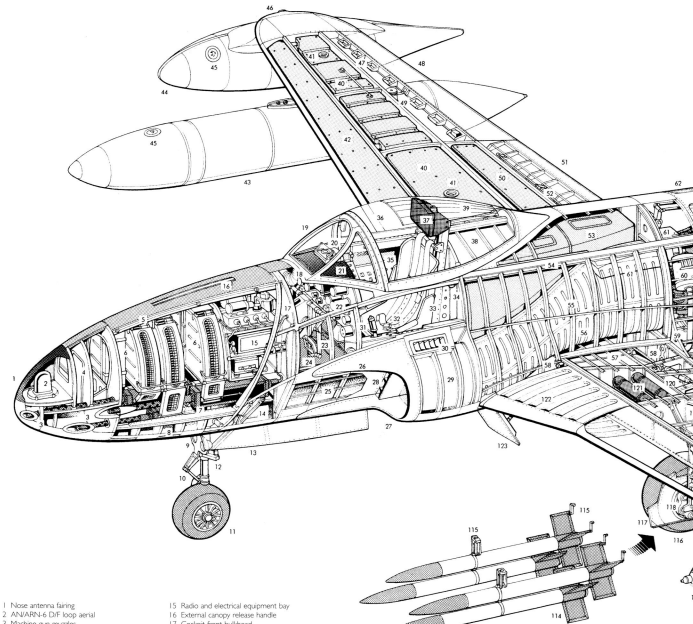

1 Nose antenna fairing	15 Radio and electrical equipment bay
2 AN/ARN-6 D/F loop aerial	16 External canopy release handle
3 Machine gun muzzles	17 Cockpit front bulkhead
4 Nose compartment frames	18 Windscreen heater duct
5 Access panel	19 Bullet-proof windscreen
6 Port and starboard ammunition boxes	20 Reflector gunsight
7 Six M-2/-3 0.5-in (12.7-mm) machine guns	21 Instrument panel shroud
8 Spent cartridge case and link ejector chute	22 Instrument panel
9 Landing and taxying lamp	23 Rudder pedals
10 Nosewheel leg torque scissors	24 Cockpit floor level
11 Nosewheel	25 Nosewheel bay
12 Steering linkage	26 Intake lip fairing
13 Nosewheel doors	27 Port air intake
14 Retraction strut	28 Boundary layer bleed air duct

29 Intake ducting	37 Ejection seat headrest
30 Boundary layer air exit louvres	38 Canopy aft decking
31 Engine throttle lever	39 Direction Finding (D/F) sense antenna
32 Safety harness	40 Starboard wing fuel tanks
33 Pilot's ejection seat	41 Fuel filler caps
34 Cockpit rear bulkhead	42 Leading edge tank
35 Starboard side console panel	43 Fletcher-type tip-tank
36 Sliding cockpit canopy cover	

44 Tip tank
45 Tip tank filler cap
46 Starboard navigation light
47 Aileron balance weights
48 Starboard aileron
49 Aileron hinge control
50 Trailing edge fuel tank
51 Starboard split trailing edge flap
52 Flap control links
53 Fuselage fuel tank
54 Fuselage main longeron
55 Centre fuselage frames
56 Intake trunking
57 Main undercarriage wheel well
58 Wing spar attachment joints
59 Pneumatic reservoir
60 Hydraulic accumulator
61 Port and starboard water injection tanks
62 Spring-loaded intake pressure relief doors
63 Allison J33-A-21 centrifugal flow turbojet engine
64 Main engine mounting
65 Rear fuselage attachments (x 3)
66 Elevator control rods
67 Jet pipe bracing cables
68 Fin root fillet
69 Elevator control link
70 Starboard tailplane
71 Starboard elevator
72 AN/ARA-8 radio homing aerial
73 AN/ARA-8 communications aerial
74 Pitot tube
75 AN/ARC-3 radio 'pick-axe' antenna
76 Rudder construction
77 Fixed tab
78 Elevator and rudder hinge controls
79 Tail navigation light
80 Jet pipe nozzle
81 Elevator tabs
82 Port elevator construction
83 Elevator mass balance
84 Tailplane construction
85 Fin/tailplane attachment points
86 Tailplane fillet fairing
87 Jet pipe mounting rail
88 Gyrosyn radio compass flux valve
89 Rear fuselage frame and stringer construction
90 Fuselage skin plating
91 Jet pipe support frame
92 Trailing edge wing root fillet
93 Flap drive motor
94 Port split trailing edge flap
95 Flap shroud ribs
96 Trailing edge fuel tank bay
97 Rear spar
98 Trailing edge ribs
99 Port aileron tab
100 Aileron hinge control
101 Upper skin panel aileron hinge line
102 Aileron construction
103 Wing tip fairing construction
104 Tip tank
105 Port navigation light
106 Tip tank mounting and jettison control
107 Detachable lower wing skin/fuel tank bay panels
108 Port wing fuel tank bays
109 Inter tank bay ribs
110 Front spar
111 Corrugated leading edge inner skin
112 Port stores pylon
113 1000-lb (454-kg) High Explosive (HE) bomb
114 5-in (12.7-cm) High-Velocity Aerial Rockets (HVARs)
115 HVAR rocket mountings
116 Port mainwheel
117 Mainwheel doors
118 Wheel brake pad
119 Main undercarriage leg strut
120 Retraction jack
121 Oxygen tanks
122 Wing root leading edge extension
123 Port ventral airbrake